CLIMATURITY

A JOURNEY INTO THE MUDDY CLIMATE MIDDLE

BY

MARC CORTEZ

CLIMATURITY.COM

Cover design by Tatiana Villa
Produced by Brian Schwartz for Wise Media Group

Rev 5.17

TABLE OF CONTENTS

GLOSSARY

Anthropogenic Warming (AGW) – is a theory explaining today's long-term increase in the average temperature of Earth's atmosphere as an effect of human industry and agriculture. This is often used interchangeably with the term 'greenhouse gas effect."

Assessment Report (AR) – the term for the climate reports written by the Intergovernmental Panel on Climate Change. The first report was published in 1990, and there have been 5 since the initial release (1995, 2001, 2007, 2015,) with AR6 released in 2022. The AR reports are generally what is referred to as The Science (regarding climate), and are used primarily to inform policymakers.

Bioenergy with Carbon Capture and Storage (BECCS) – is the process of extracting energy from biomass and capturing and storing the carbon, thereby removing it from the atmosphere. The carbon in the biomass comes from the (CO_2) which is extracted from the atmosphere by the biomass when it grows. Some of the carbon in the biomass is converted to CO_2 or biochar which can then be stored by geologic sequestration or land application, enabling carbon dioxide removal (CDR).

Biomass – is plant-based material used as fuel to produce heat or electricity. Examples are wood and wood residues, energy crops, agricultural residues, and waste from industry, farms and households.

Carbon capture and storage (CCS) – also known as carbon capture and sequestration, is the process of capturing carbon dioxide (CO_2) before it enters the atmosphere, transporting it, and storing it (sequestration).

Carbon cycle – the carbon cycle describes the process in which carbon atoms continually travel from the atmosphere to the Earth and then back into the atmosphere. Since our planet and its atmosphere form a closed environment, the amount of carbon in this system does not change. Where the carbon is located — in the atmosphere or on Earth — is constantly in flux.

Carbon dioxide (CO_2) – Carbon dioxide is a chemical compound that occurs naturally in Earth's atmosphere as a trace gas. Atmospheric CO_2 is the primary carbon source for life on Earth. Plants, algae and cyanobacteria use energy from sunlight to synthesize carbohydrates from carbon dioxide and water in a process called photosynthesis, which produces oxygen as a waste product. Since plants require CO_2 for photosynthesis, and humans and animals depend on plants for food, CO_2 is necessary for the survival of life on earth.

Carbon negative – carbon negative is the state of removing more CO_2 emissions than one emits, thereby achieving a negative carbon balance. Since it's not possible to negatively emit CO_2, this term refers to the overall accounting of one's carbon footprint.

Carbon neutral – carbon neutral is the state of zero carbon emissions, which can be achieved by lowering one's emissions or offsetting emissions with other carbon-absorbing techniques.

Carbon sequestration – carbon sequestration is the process of capturing and storing atmospheric CO_2. Geologic carbon sequestration is the process of storing carbon dioxide (CO_2) in underground geologic formations., while biologic sequestration is the process of storing CO_2 in vegetation, soils, woody products, and aquatic environments.

Climaccounting – is a term used to describe creative and questionable accounting methods used to assign benefits and blames to various climate solutions. Climaccounting is a way to make one preferred climate option more attractive than another. Creative accounting, wrongful attribution, guesses-taken-as-givens, incomplete data, inadequate comparisons, and selective omissions are all climaccounting techniques.

Climaturity – is a term used to advocate for an open, transparent, and pragmatic approach to solving our climate problems. It acknowledges climate change is real, mankind has had some influence on it, and aims to solve it through real, pragmatic solutions.

Climate deather – also known as climate alarmist or climate panicker, it's a pseudonym for hardcore environmentalists who believe and promote an aggressive climate apocalypse narrative.

Climate denier – a pseudonym for those who do not believe in mankind's climate influence and deny that it's a critical problem that should be solved.

Concentrating Solar Power (CSP) – refers to a solar electricity generation technique that uses mirrors to concentrate (focus) the sun's light energy and convert it into heat to create steam to drive a turbine that generates electrical power.

Direct Air Capture (DAC) - is a technological method that uses chemical reactions to capture CO_2 from the atmosphere. When air moves over these chemicals, they selectively react with and remove CO_2, allowing the other components of air to pass through. These chemicals can take the form of either liquid solvents or solid sorbents, which make up the two types of DAC systems in use today. The captured CO_2 can be injected underground for permanent storage in certain geologic formations or used in various products and applications.

Electric vehicle (EV) – a vehicle that is powered by electricity and not by fossil fuels.

Environmental Protection Agency (EPA) – The Environmental Protection Agency is a United States federal government agency whose mission is to protect human and environmental health. The EPA regulates the manufacturing, processing, distribution, and use of chemicals and other pollutants. The agency enforces its findings through fines, sanctions, and other procedures, and oversees programs to promote energy efficiency, environmental stewardship, sustainable growth, air and water quality, and pollution prevention.

Gigawatt (GW) – refers to one billion watts of electricity generation capacity, or 1,000,000,000 watts.

Greenhouse Gases (GHGs) – GHGs are gasses that absorb and emit radiant energy, causing the greenhouse effect. The primary GHGs in the Earth's atmosphere are water vapor (H_2O), CO_2, methane (CH_4), nitrous oxide (N_2O), and ozone (O_3). Without GHGs, the average earth temperature would be much lower than it currently is, due to the greenhouse gas effect. The greenhouse gas effect is a process that occurs when energy from a planet's sun goes through its atmosphere and warms the planet's surface, but the atmosphere prevents the heat from returning directly to space, resulting in a warmer planet

Gross Domestic Product (GDP) – an economic metric that measures a country's economic activity and health. It is a measure of the monetary value of goods and services produced by a country over a specific period of time.

Hydropower – or hydroelectricity, is the means of producing electricity by flowing water over blades to turn electricity-producing generators.

Intergovernmental Panel on Climate Change (IPCC) – is the United Nations body for assessing the science related to climate change.

Kilowatt-hour (kWh) – refers to the amount of electricity produced by one kilowatt for one hour.

Megawatt (MW) – refers to one million watts of electricity generation capacity, or 1,000,000 watts.

National Oceanographic and Atmospheric Administration (NOAA) – NOAA is an American scientific and regulatory agency within the U.S. Department of Commerce that forecasts weather, monitors oceanic and atmospheric conditions, charts the seas, conducts deep sea exploration, and manages fishing and protection of marine mammals and endangered species in the U.S. exclusive economic zone.

Net zero – see carbon neutral.

Photovoltaic (PV) – more commonly known as solar panels, PV generates power using devices that absorb energy from sunlight and convert it into electrical energy. These devices, known as solar cells, are then connected to form larger power-generating units known as modules or panels.

Psyence – a term used to describe the practice of using science-infused computer models to generate doomsday climate scenarios that can manipulate public perception and policy. Also known as propaganda.

Terrawatt (TW) – refers to one trillion watts of electricity generation capacity, or 1,000,000,000,000 watts.

INTRODUCTION

Why write this book? That's the question I keep getting from my renewable energy colleagues. They say, "You spent 23 years in cleantech, so why throw wrenches now?"

Well, if wanting the truth is throwing wrenches, then maybe it's already too late.

There seems to be only two sides in the climate discussion. On one side are the climate deathers who believe our planet's heating atmosphere is leading to human extinction. On the other side are the climate deniers who believe that all's-fine-and-there's-nothing-to-worry-about-here. Try having a conversation with someone on either side and you'll see what I mean.

Most of us, however, lie somewhere in the climate middle between those two extremes. We believe the planet is warming and that mankind has had some impact on it, yet we don't know how serious it really is. We're told by the climate media that we're dying, yet we're not. We're told by climate scientists that their models accurately predict the future, yet they're wrong every time. We know it's a different type of science—one that uses models to predict the future instead of tests that prove scientific certainty—yet no one explains the difference and why we should believe it. We're told by our leaders that we're in the midst of an existential crisis right before they board their gas-fueled jets and call OPEC to deliver more oil. They scare our children, then celebrate their fear on magazine covers. We're told the debate is over and when we ask questions we're yelled at, labeled, ostracized, and bullied. Then, we're handed the bill to fix the problems.

Above all, no one is telling the full truth, and we know it. This is no way to fix a global problem.

I've spent nearly 25 years on the front lines of the climate battle and have worked hard to solve our climate problems. I've worked for and built companies in solar, electric vehicles, energy storage, and now water conservation. In short, I've fought the good fight. I, along with my colleagues and competitors, were united in the fight towards a better climate future, and I'm proud to have worked on the climate front lines for as long as I have.

But the climate death narrative has changed the dynamic and screeched climate progress to a halt. We've let the climate deathers steal the bullhorn, creating blueprints to scare us, strategies to sue us, and campaigns to tax us. As a university professor, I deal with these after-effects daily: young adults suffering from acute eco-anxiety, the suppressive feeling that our climate journey is hopeless and that their children will likely die from runaway climate change. And so I ask: How did we fail our children so miserably?

Enough.

Those of us in the climate middle believe that our climate problem is real but not terminal, and we genuinely want to solve it in a practical, pragmatic, and affordable way. We are willing to make sacrifices and do what's best for the planet once we understand the real problem, solving it in ways that don't reverse mankind's economic and societal progress. We're on board with it once we stop being yelled at, labeled, hated, manipulated, lied to and pick pocketed. We want a plan to attack climate change head-on, one that most of our country can get behind.

While I am an engineer and businessman who has spent decades building climate solutions, I am not a climate scientist.

The opinions I express herein are mine, and the questions I ask have been formed over years working in the industry. Many of you will find fault with my analysis of the science and the opinions I derive from them, and I'm fine with that. I would love for you to do your own research, develop your own opinions, and create counterarguments to everything I've said. In fact, I encourage you to do just that.

We need everybody's eyes and ears on this critical problem. We're being handed a whopping multi-trillion-dollar bill to fix it, so we as Americans have both a right and responsibility to ask these questions.

Please join me in crafting a new climate narrative, one where we can carve a new path down the middle with open dialog, pragmatic thinking, and forward-looking solutions.

Please join me in creating a new era of *Climaturity*.

~MC

CHAPTER 1
INTRODUCTION

We are being told that climate change is the biggest problem we will ever face in our lifetime. We are being told it's the biggest problem our children and grandchildren will face. It's a crisis, it's an emergency, and if we don't do something about it *now*, humanity is in danger. Forever.

And yet, are we really willing to take the necessary actions change it? Are we willing to sacrifice our children's college funds, to give up reliable energy, to reverse our entire way of life in order to tackle climate change on? If not, why?

Maybe it's because we don't really believe it's an actual emergency.

If you had a heart attack, you'd be rushed to the hospital. If you were critical, your family would rush to your side. If the doctors said you needed expensive surgery, you'd spend your life savings on the procedure. And you would certainly adopt the lifestyle changes your doctor recommended going forward. In short, you would change your life immediately to respond to the emergency—because it's a real emergency.

How many of us have done the same for climate change? I can only speak for myself. Out of the last $1000 I've spent, most of it has been for my home, food, my children's college fund, new lacrosse equipment, my anniversary dinner, and a dental appointment. Oh, I did buy a homeless man a sandwich, and I bought some community solar. So, I guess that makes me feel a bit better. But I didn't spend any money to save the melting Himalayas.

Hey, before you yell at me, did you? Are you saving 20% of your annual income to prepare for the pending climate catastrophe or did you rush to buy a Volt while it was still cheap? Have you invested your kid's college fund into high-ground real estate to protect yourselves from the upcoming global floods, or did you go to Whole Foods to buy organic food? Are you installing solar now, or are you waiting for prices to drop? What did *you* do this week to prevent Manhattan from flooding?

Probably nothing. When it comes down to it, we're all making daily, practical, economic decisions. We're doing what we have to do for our families and our local communities. Does that make us selfish? Of course. We all work towards our self-interests, and it's I to think naïve otherwise. Just today you made a decision that benefited you and yours only. So did I. We only have so much money and time to spend on our lives, so we do the best we can with that. If we have an extra 50 cents to save the planet at the end of our days, then we will, but if I have to choose between my kid's college and the Himalayas, I'll choose college every single time. And so will you.

If we truly believed that we only have a few years left until the world begins its irreversible decline, we'd be acting differently. We are not acting as if we're in a true emergency, because we're not. Instead, we're doing simple, affordable things. We buy solar systems and electric vehicles and organic foods. We clap when teenage activists scold the United Nations for a lack of climate urgency, and we tweet the Children for Climate protests to our social media friends to show we care. ("By golly, isn't scaring our children the right thing to do? You betcha!") We yell at climate-denying Republicans because, well, we can, and it sure retweets well. It's easy to blame them because *they're* really the problem.

Let's be honest with ourselves. We want the global climate change problem to be solved as long as we don't have to make great sacrifices to make it happen. At the end of the day, we'll sacrifice a polar bear or two in order to put our kids through college, because those are the real choices we make. The 2019 Davos Conference welcomed 1500 private jet flights into Switzerland to talk about climate change, releasing countless CO_2 emissions into the air, but hey, they sure did talk about important stuff. Maybe they felt guilty about it afterwards, but they did it anyway.

Maybe instead of climate change being Stage 4 cancer, it's more like the 10 pounds we gained after Thanksgiving dinner. Is it really an emergency, or is it just extra weight we have to sweat off before Christmas?

Is climate change a real emergency or more like the extra weight you have to sweat off after Thanksgiving?

CHAPTER 2
WELCOME TO THE
INTERGOVERNMENTAL PANEL
ON CLIMATE CHANGE

The Intergovernmental Panel on Climate Change (IPCC) is a body of the United Nations whose charter is to cover the "scientific, technical and socio-economic information relevant to understanding the scientific basis of risk of human-induced climate change, its potential impacts and options for adaptation and mitigation."[1] It does not conduct primary research, nor does it monitor the climate itself. Its job is to evaluate and offer science and opinions created by other people in order to influence policy. While thousands of scientists contribute their research to the IPCC process, the IPCC's job is to review and create scenarios and assessments of the state of climate science. They simply frame what they're being told.

As an arm of the UN, the IPCC is by its very nature a political body. Since its formation in 1988, the IPCC has produced six Climate Assessment Reports, the first in 1990 and the latest in 2021. While each Assessment Report contains thousands of pages (AR6 2021 is a whopping 3,949 pages), they also produce a Summary Report for Policymakers during each report cycle that summarizes their findings.

In general, the IPCC AR reports are what people and politicians refer to as "The Science." The now-infamous 97% scientific consensus comes from the IPCC. In terms of our climate discussion, the IPCC AR reports are considered The Bible.

Each report analyzes thousands of primary climate research reports, then creates scenarios with which to frame our future-looking discussions (more on scenarios and modeling later). The analyst group compiles results from 3 separate working groups— science, impacts, and mitigation—and were originally chartered to present a full range of scenarios, without regard to probability of each scenario happening. As Roger Pielke said in this *Forbes* 2019 article:

> At the time the IPCC recognized that 'the future is inherently unpredictable and so views will differ as to which of the storylines and representative scenarios could be more or less likely. Therefore, the development of a single 'best guess' or 'business-as-usual' scenario is neither desirable nor possible . . . the term 'business-as-usual' may be misleading and most climate scenarios considered in this report can be regarded as exploratory.[2]

They created 40 different emission scenarios—each with different assumptions about future greenhouse gas pollution, land use, and other factors—and grouped those into 4 separate families. They also made assumptions about future technological and economic development.[3],[4]

The family of A1 scenarios, for example, highlights a world with rapid economic growth, global population of 9 billion by 2050 (that subsequently declines), a quick spread of new and efficient technologies, and a tightly integrated world with extensive global and cultural interactions. By contrast, the B1 scenario family highlights a more service and information-focused global economy, introductions of clean and resource efficient technologies, and an emphasis on global solutions to economic, social, and environmental stability. RPC scenario 8.5, a scenario that has gained global notoriety, includes a 98% percentile carbon emissions outlook, slower technological growth, and high population growth (more on RPC 8.5 later).

These exploratory scenarios depict dozens of outcomes that are equally possible, and they openly acknowledge the many uncertainties, as well as our own inherent ignorance, of the future. Now, imagine all of those scenarios laid before you in a 40-cell matrix. Notice anything similar about them?

They are all guesses.

Of course, they are all smart guesses, based on the assumptions of scientists and global policy professionals. These are experts at what they do; there is no better group of people to create these scenarios. They've studied the world's economies, climates, politics, social trends, and made assumptions about hundreds of factors and how they might evolve over the years. All of the scenarios represent "neutral" points of view: they don't predict future disasters or catastrophes or wars or environmental collapses; and they don't judge whether any of the pathways are good or bad. Smart though they are, they are all speculations into the future.

Why is this analysis so critical?

It's important because all of our climate perspectives—all of our talking points and arguments and government policies—start from this 40-comparment matrix of guesses. We are literally using a spreadsheet of potential future predictions to decide whether or not we'll spend trillions of dollars.

Think about that for a moment: Global Climate Policy is based on an invented spreadsheet we populate with invented numbers for invented scenarios. And how do we generate the numbers for these 40 scenarios? Computer models.

~~~~~~~~~~~

To frame this discussion, let's use a scientific continuum to evaluate how climate modeling compares to physical, empirical science.

If we created a big Science-O-Meter with a graded 0 -10 scale on it—with 10 being physical science, and 0 being pure speculation—we could rank the different factors and see how it all lays out. It's subjective, of course, and certainly not definitive, but at least it provides a way to compare each factor's relative scientific validity.

Climate models are complex and require inputs of dozens of variables. Some of the input factors are science-based, but most of them are educated guesses. Let's look at some of the climate factors that go into the models.

Model Factor 1: Temperatures.

Climate scientists have been measuring global temperatures for thousands of years, and it's what most people refer to when they think of climate science. Prior to 12,000 years ago, temperatures were analyzed using paleoclimate, ice cores, and geologic evidence and observations. In 1850, we were able to begin actual measurements of temperatures using thermometers, and since 1950 we added satellites and balloons into the measurement mix. In our current climate discussions, most of the pertinent information refers to temperatures after 1850. The graph in figure 1 shows, in general, the results of that data.

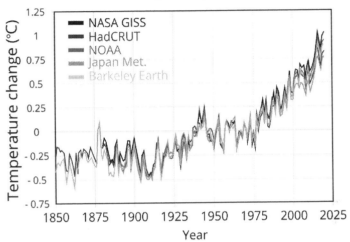

Figure 1. Global Temperatures Over Time[5]

I'll leave the debate about the relative validity of paleoclimate analysis vs. satellite measurements to others much more able to debate the factors. The point of presenting the data is to show what type of information is publicly available to frame our discussion.[6]

Temperature measurements are great for charting our previous temperature path, but that doesn't mean they can predict the future. Charting temperatures from our past is empirical but projecting those temperatures into the future is speculation.

On the Science-O-Meter we invented a few paragraphs ago, past temperature measurements are probably about an 8 on a science scale of 10, while projecting those temperatures into the future are about a 2. This distinction is important.

Model Factor 2: Rising CO_2 levels.

As you might expect, the measurement and accounting of CO_2 levels over time has come under intense scrutiny. Primarily reliant on ice-core analysis dating back thousands of years, tracking and predicting CO_2 levels is a foundation of climate science. Without diving too deeply into the debate, here are 2 graphs that show some CO_2 measurements over time.

As you can see, the curves look quite different depending upon the scale shown: some argue that CO_2 levels now are an extension of previous cycles[7], while others argue that current CO_2 levels are unprecedented and are due to man's industrial revolution impacts. For the purposes of our discussion, we'll say that we can indeed show rising CO_2 levels[8].

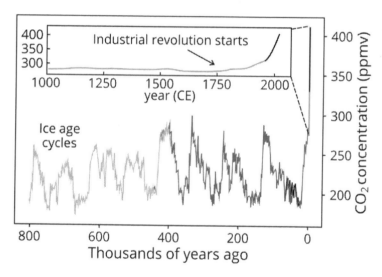

Figure 2. CO_2 Levels Over Time

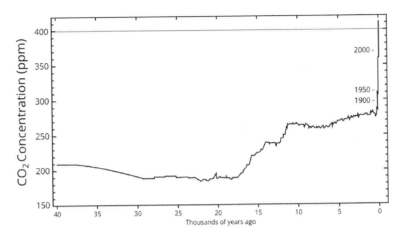

Figure 3. CO_2 Levels Over Time, Alternate View

Given what we know about previous CO_2 analysis and current CO_2 measurements, we can give rising CO_2 levels about a 7 or 8 on our Science-O-Meter.

Model Factor 3: Does CO_2 cause temperature rise, or does temperature rise cause CO_2 rise?

Another fundamental assumption in the entire climate discussion is the idea that rising CO_2 levels cause temperatures to rise, which means that our main priority should be controlling manmade CO_2 levels. Indeed, if this assumption is not true, then the entire man-is-causing-the-entire-world-to-heat argument falls apart. If ever there was a need for hard, physical science that proves rising CO_2 directly causes rising temperatures this is the place, isn't it?

Well yes, but unfortunately the science gets a bit slippery.

A graph from the National Oceanic and Atmospheric Administration (NOAA), shows the link between temperatures and CO_2, and says: "The strong *correspondence* [emphasis added] between temperature and concentration of carbon dioxide in the atmosphere during …the past several hundred thousand years."

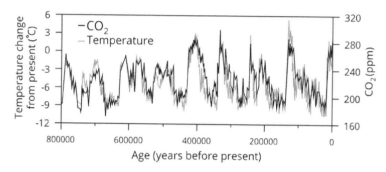

Figure 4. CO_2 and Temperature Relationship Over Time

NOAA continues: "While it might seem simple to determine cause and effect between carbon dioxide and climate from which change occurs first, or from some other means, the determination of cause and effect remains exceedingly difficult."[9]

Hmm, not exactly scientific proof, is it?

Actually, the "phase lag" of CO_2 rising after temperature rise has been happening for thousands of years and is something science has been able to prove. According to a 2013 study[10]; the "concentration of CO_2 in the atmosphere follows the rise in Antarctic temperatures very closely and is staggered by a few hundred years," a conclusion that has been discussed extensively in the media and is not disputed. Even Joe Barton, a congressman from Texas, drove the point home by testifying: "An article in *Science* magazine illustrated that a rise in carbon dioxide did not precede a rise in temperatures, but actually lagged behind temperature rises by 200 to 1000 years. A rise in carbon dioxide levels could not have caused a rise in temperature if it followed the temperature."[11]

In response, those who disagree say that "this statement does not tell the whole story,[12]" and that: "This is ONLY true BEFORE the Industrial Revolution (IR). Before the IR, humans were not emitting CO_2 to the atmosphere so only natural changes could have caused CO_2 changes and these changes occurred over thousands of years.[13]"

For thousands of years CO_2 lagged temperature rise, but the Industrial Revolution reversed that trend? Any real science to prove that?

Nope.

It's process-of-elimination-attribution-science: If rising temperatures caused CO_2 rise before, then the inclusion of a new element (namely us, and the Industrial Revolution) must reverse that trend because what else could it be? Those were facts before, now it's different. Until it's not.

A 2012 study found that, even after man's post-Industrial-Age CO_2 emission spree, CO_2 rise lagged temperature rise by 9-12 months—still less than the years before, but still…lagging. The study also delivered this whopper: "As cause must always precede effect, this observation demonstrates that modern changes in temperatures are generally not induced by changes in atmospheric CO_2. Indeed, the sequence of events is seen to be the opposite: temperature changes are taking place before the corresponding CO_2 changes occur."[14]

Wait. Say that again.

"The sequence of events is seen to be the opposite: temperature changes are taking place before the corresponding CO_2 changes occur."

If science can't prove causation between CO_2 and temperatures, then what the hell are we talking about? If this is a big scientific unknown, then the entire future-looking climate equation gets a lot more speculative, doesn't it?

On the Science-O-Meter, the links between rising manmade emissions and rising CO_2 and rising global temperatures is about a five.

Model Factor 4: Country decarbonization plans.

The IPCC scenarios include current emission pathways using today's current renewable energy mix, all the way up to a renewable energy penetration of 66%. Never mind that current global capacity is microscopic compared to a 66% renewable penetration. These are pure, what-if estimates.

Any science here? Nope. On our science scale, this is a 0.

Model Factor 5: Country's economic activities (GDP).

See Model Factor 3, on a country's decarbonization plans. A 0 on the science scale. Pure estimates. And on and on.

Now, for each square of the matrix, you fill in the blank with an estimate. Climate models attempt to estimate factors such as: future temperature changes, future mix of Greenhouse Gases (GHGs), the growth and change of those GHGs over time, the growth of each individual contributor of GHGs, how those individual contributors change over time, man's contribution to those GHGs, how that will change over time...in addition to dozens of other scenarios. On the socioeconomic side, you're trying to estimate regional and global Gross Domestic Product (GDP) growth over time, regional and global population growth, and resettlement and population migration likelihoods, to name a few. And then there are the energy alternatives: a continuation of today's fossil fuel business as usual, an assumption of our global alternative energy adoption rate over time, an assumption of the mix of that alternative energy rate and its growth over time.

Quickly now: What is Mozambique's GDP going to be in 2034? What is France's renewable energy adoption rate going to be in 2030? What is America's population going to be in 2045? Feel good about all those numbers?

That is our climate modeling process. Of the dozens of variables we input into the system, 2 or 3 contain empirical science content, while the rest consist of assumptions and estimates. Even if the entire equation contains some real, physical science, when that model is multiplied by dozens of other estimates the entire output becomes, by definition, an estimate. Science input becomes scientific theory and is used to present what-if scenarios. One bit of science sprinkled in with fifty bits of estimates becomes lost in an ocean of assumptions. True science gets swallowed up into calculated conjecture. Said another way: Gravity can be proven with physical science and is a scientific fact. Climate predictions can be infused with scientific data but can only produce conjectures.

Before we leave the climate modeling discussion, we need to ask the trillion-dollar question: How correct are these models? Like usual, it depends upon whom you ask, and like usual, it turns political. Outlets from the left will typically say that the climate models are "reasonably accurate" while outlets from the right point out how wrong they are.

The Daily Mail said: "Climate change models may not have been accurate after all as study finds most widely overestimated global warming."[15]

ScienceMag.org said: "New climate models predict a warming surge."[16]

For example, Vox said that: "Scientists have gotten predictions of global warming right since the 1970s" and acknowledges that models are "complicated" but "generally quite accurate"; but that "how human societies and technologies develop, which depends on endless variables that climate scientists can't possibly be expected to predict...it's not fair to blame the models when those projections of forcings turn out to be mistaken."[17] The Cato Institute issued a "Closer Look at a Lukewarming World" report that says "There is strong evidence that the climate models predict too much warming".[18]

The CO_2 Coalition, a group of climate scientists, policy makers, and thought leaders, goes all-in on CO_2's positive benefits: "More carbon dioxide levels will help everyone, including future generations of our families. CO_2 is the essential food for land-based plants. The Earth's biosphere has experienced a relative CO_2 famine for millions of years, and the recent increase in CO_2 levels has had a measurable, positive effect on plant life."[19]

Media coverage down the center aisle is also mixed. A 2017 *CarbonBrief* article entitled "How well have climate models projected global warming?" analyzed 5 predictive reports, with mixed results:

- "His warming estimate of 0.6°C was nearly spot-on" but the CO_2 estimate was "overestimated."
- "Broecker's projected warming was reasonably close to observations for a few decades, but recently has been considerably higher."
- "The overall rate of warming between 1970 and 2016 projected by Hansen et al. in 1981 in the fast-growth scenario has been about 20% lower than observations...scenario B projected a rate of warming between 1970 and 2016 that was approximately 30% higher than what has been observed."[20]

Even a 2017 *Forbes* article[21] says that older climate models "got almost everything exactly right", but acknowledges that:

"Models have been very effective in predicting climate change, but have not been as effective in predicting its impact on ecosystem[s] and human society. The distinction between the two has not been stated clearly."

There you have it. In the end, what you believe probably depends on what you already believe.

The IPCC creates what-if scenarios and uses computer models to try and predict our climate future. They do not conduct primary climate research.

CHAPTER 3
PHYSICAL OR MODELED SCIENCE?

Read any good Climate Science lately? Me either. Well, I've read some—more than many, less than others—but it's not an easy task. I genuinely want to learn what is real and what is not, so I've gone searching for the science. But finding it is not easy, and usually what I find instead are other publications interpreting the science and telling me how and what to think.

Over the past 6 months I've asked my network this exact question. I know hundreds of people in solar, electric vehicles, energy, tech startups and the investment community, and if anyone could help clarify this it would be this group. So far, I've asked over a hundred people if they've read *any* climate research, and the results are surprising. Of all the people I asked, how many have read some actual climate science?

Eight.

Really.

I am in no way criticizing anyone. They are true believers and have worked on the front lines of the cleantech industry for decades; these people have literally built the industries we're now turning to for climate solutions. And yet most of us have not read the actual science: I myself have read a few different reports and they are very difficult to understand for non-climate-scientist folk.

The truth is that most of us get climate science information not from the science itself but rather from the various media outlets we read, which means we're reading someone else's opinion about the climate, which also means we're absorbing their bias. If you're true climate believers then you read the IPCC reports, but as we've seen, those are written by analysts who work for governments and politicians—not scientists.

Even in my very unscientific poll, less than 10% of the people had read the actual science, and this is among my network of informed climate front-liners. In the general population, that number is undoubtedly much less.

The Most Convenient Truth is that whenever someone says, "It's about the science, stupid," there's a very good chance that they've never actually read any of the science.

One of the most basic questions within the entire climate discussions is "Hey, is predictive climate science the same as provable, physical science?"

Well, no. Models that try and predict the future are different than measurable, observable phenomena we can study in labs. They both exist on the science spectrum, but they have different purposes and results, and it's important to recognize and understand the differences.

Back when I was in engineering school, I was taught the scientific method and was required to use it to physically prove things. In short, the scientific method was: (1) develop a hypothesis about something, (2) develop a way to test for it in a controlled environment, (3) run the test, (4) evaluate the results against your hypothesis, then (5) rerun the tests. We were taught that physical science was something that can be proven over and over again.

Using the scientific method, things like gravity and physics can be proven and replicated by scientists everywhere. Results are timeless and replicable and form the basis of our scientific foundation. Physical science is, mostly importantly, indisputable. There is no voting within the physical sciences. It's simply a scientific fact or it isn't.

Scientific theory, on the other hand, uses physical laws to push the boundaries of science and scientific thinking in order to exercise "What if?" scenarios. The goal of scientific theory is to push the discussion forward and give us food for thought, but because it is theoretical, it isn't constrained by burdens of proof. Albert Einstein and his Theory of Relativity certainly pushed forward scientific thought, but the only proof of going faster-than-the-speed-of-light is in Star Wars.

The distinction between measurable, physical science, and climate scientific theory has been blurred by the climate media and politicians to the point of irrelevance. They have pretended that these are the same, but they are not. Most of the misunderstanding about climate science is because of these fundamental differences.

Those who believe in our imminent climate destruction believe that predictive climate models hold scientific certainty and highlight the oft-touted "scientific consensus" as proof. Those who minimize mankind's climate effects believe that true science requires physical proof and direct causation and that future-looking models are junk science and proof of nothing. Whichever side you're on, it's easy to dismiss the other side because of these differences in understanding. This is not a trivial thing, and opinions are far from settled within the scientific community.

Dr. Richard Lindzen, retired MIT astrophysicist and contributing IPCC scientist, said, "The global warming issue parts company with normative science at an early stage," and observes that "This clearly is of no importance to the thousands of…bureaucrats and advocates whose livelihood is tied to climate alarmism."[22] While acknowledging that climate science shows the planet is warming, Dr. Lindzen clearly stated that there is a big difference between normative and climate science.

In response, Dr. Stefan Rahmstorf, a climatologist, Professor at Potsdam University and one of the IPCC's lead contributors, disagreed with Dr. Lindzen. Dr. Rahmstorf's asserted that manmade global warming is a given and that the scientific consensus is valid. He made no distinction between the two types of science.

The IPCC itself acknowledges these differences, and their reports include confidence language within their scenarios. They developed a set of probabilities that readers could use to help understand the scientific validity of their claims. For example, if something is "likely", that means it has a >66% chance of that factor occurring. Something "about as likely as not" has between a 33 and 66% of that factor occurring, and so on. Yes, there are some factors that have a "virtually certain" or >99% occurrence of that factor happening, but there are others that are "exceptionally unlikely".

Those handicaps clearly demonstrate the differences between physical science and climate science. The paper in which they produced these is called "The IPCC's evaluation of evidence and treatment of uncertainty."[23] They have literally created a legend on how to handicap their climate predictions.

The point is not to decide which of the thousands of climate scientists are right or wrong, but simply to highlight that the types of science they all engage in are different. They are not the same. I doubt that Drs. Lindzen and Rahmstorf would disagree about the existence of gravity, but they certainly disagree about the soft science of global warming. Which type is correct? Even they can't agree.

So, how many scientific studies prove that we are headed towards ecological disaster? None. And how many models show we could be headed towards ecological disaster? As many as we want to show. And therein lies the rub.

CHAPTER 4
CLIMATE PSYENCE, AND
OTHER TRICKS OF THE TRADE

Science: knowledge about or study of the natural world based on facts learned through experiments and observation.

—Merriam-Webster Dictionary[24]

Psyence: 1) the use of science-infused computer models to sway public opinion about climate scenarios; 2) propaganda.

—M. Cortez

By now we've seen the climate planning process, the science involved, and the modeling techniques used to create and exercise the various climate scenarios. Despite what we've heard, the science is not settled, from the temperature measurements and techniques used all the way to the economic and societal assumptions we've created. Over the decades our understanding of the climate has increased, and even though that knowledge has been captured in updated models, they are still smart, future-looking guesses. Each scenario is, by definition, fiction and should be treated as such.

Therein lies our opportunity, but also our biggest danger.

Those who believe in the IPCC reports as scientific fact can view them as the de facto climate Bible, to be followed and propagated as the ultimate solution. Any questions about the reports' efficacy and validity can be filled in by blind faith and, in many cases, an almost religious fanaticism.

Those who acknowledge empirical science as the only type of valid science will view the IPPC reports as yet more government-fueled propaganda pushing forward an expensive and misplaced agenda. Which of those two opposite narratives you follow probably depends on your reaction to climate psyence.

In military terms, PsyOps are "Operations to convey selected information and indicators to audiences to influence their emotions, motives, and objective reasoning, and ultimately the behavior of governments, organizations, groups, and individuals." Tools of PsyOps campaigns include propaganda, communication systems, videos and production centers, and other means to create and disseminate critical messaging.

Climate psyence is PsyOps to conduct climate warfare, and it's used by scientists, politicians, analysts, and media outlets to sway public opinion.

When Big Oil hires independent analysts to create false narratives decoupling oil use from climate change, that's psyence; the Koch Brothers do the same. When Al Gore produces a movie that shows Manhattan flooding by 2100, that's psyence. When President Trump calls climate change a hoax, that's psyence. When TIME magazine puts Greta Thunberg on their cover as 2019 Person of the Year, that's psyence. When

Facebook and Twitter and LinkedIn remove questions about manmade climate change from their sites, that's psyence. When Joe Biden calls to spend trillions on jobs and healthcare programs under the name of The Green New Deal, that's psyence.

The magic of psyence is that there is actually some level of science inside each argument. It doesn't have to be feasible (seriously, does anyone think Manhattan is *really* going to flood out?), it just has to sound somewhat possible. The point is to snag people with emotional hooks to trigger their fears and insecurities, so they can be more easily manipulated.

Is that sinister? Maybe, but it's also Marketing 101: target an audience's insecurities and offer readily available solutions to alleviate these insecurities. Marketing aims to create an emotional reaction which in turn aims to create money. Solve someone's pain, and they'll fund your solution. Real pain is preferable, but manufactured pain is a close second.

Big Oil and the Koch Family use psyence to make sure you continue to buy their products. Al Gore uses psyence to help sway Congress for his climate-spending programs when he's President. Or to give his election loss some gravitas. Or to have people spend on his Generation Investment Fund portfolio. Or all three. President Trump uses psyence to make sure oil people continue to vote for him. Joe Biden uses psyence to make sure green people continue to vote for him. And on and on and on.

As we can see, using marquee names to develop and communicate the messages is one of the first items in the psyence toolkit.

Perhaps the most notable celebrity-politician to push his version of climate psyence was Al Gore, with his movie *An Inconvenient Truth*. In May of 2006, as Mr. Gore was promoting his film, he conducted an online Grist interview where he said:

"I believe it is appropriate to have an over-representation of factual presentations on how dangerous it is."[25]

Of course, the movie trailers and posters claimed it would be "The scariest movie you'll ever see!" And when people went to see the movie, they were greeted by those "over-representation of factual presentations" about climate change.

Clunky language aside, Mr. Gore produced a movie that exaggerated facts with doom and gloom predictions. He chose to present those death predictions instead of less apocalyptic ones, cherry-picked from the dozens of scenarios presented in the IPCC reports. He sprinkled in enough facts to give it credibility, then made the rest of it up. He helped create the climapocalypse, leveraged his big media marquee value, and created a long list of disciples. His movie was his opinion, nothing more, and the world of true believers was only happy to follow along.

Extinction Rebellion, an environmental activist group, cited "mass extinction" and that "life on earth is in crisis"[26] on their website. Bill McKibben, a well-known environmental activist, tweeted his suggestion that Australian climate fires have effectively made koalas "functionally extinct."[27] *Vice* published an article entitled: "The Collapse of Civilization May Have Already Begun."[28] Alexandria Ocasio-Cortez, a congresswoman from New York, gave an interview to USA Today and said: "The world is going to going to end in 12 years" and described climate change as her generation's "World War II."[29]

Ms. Greta Thunberg, a Swedish teenager turned climate activist, was so devoted to the climate death message that she took a sailboat across the Atlantic to speak at the United Nations, where she trended on Twitter, headlined on CNN, The New York Times, The Washington Post, and loads of other mainstream media outlets. She missed school every week for her

"Fridays for Future" protests and headed up a global children's climate-protest movement; she spanned the globe scolding adults of our impending climate disaster. She stared right into the CNN cameras and told us all we should be ashamed of ourselves.

Not to be outdone, the IPCC analysts whose earliest charter was to present science and opinions fairly, abandoned these principles in favor of an agenda they wanted to push. In 1989, one year before the IPCC issued their first assessment report, the United Nations issued a climate alarm press release that said:

> [Director of the New York office of the UNEP, Noel Brown] says entire nations could be wiped off the face of the Earth by rising sea levels if the global warming trend is not reversed by the year 2000. ... He said governments have a 10-year window of opportunity to solve the greenhouse effect before it goes beyond human control.[30]

Twenty-two years later a scientific review noted the "UNEP had already decided, even before the first IPCC report in 1990, that humans were to blame for climate change through their greenhouse gas emissions."[31] In other words, UNEP's position was that mankind caused global warming, and they set about to produce a report and infrastructure that proved it. One way to strengthen the validity of this so-called science is to suppress those who don't agree with this perspective.

Those same scientists doubled down on their critique of UNEP's unilateralism in their 2021 study,[32] noting that:

> One factor that we believe is highly relevant is the fact that a primary goal of the IPCC reports is to "speak with one voice for climate science." *This drive to present a single "scientific consensus" on issues has...been achieved by suppressing*

dissenting views on any issues where there is still scientific disagreement [emphasis added]. As a result, an accurate knowledge of those issues where there is ongoing scientific dissensus (and why) is often missing from the IPCC reports. This is concerning for policy makers relying on the IPCC reports because... "*the consensus approach deprives policy makers of a full view of the plurality of scientific opinions within and between the various scientific disciplines that study the climate problem* [emphasis added]" From our perspective as members of the scientific community, we are also concerned that this suppression of open-minded scientific inquiry may be hindering scientific progress into improving our understanding of these challenging issues.

With a goal of presenting a unified approach to policymakers, the IPCC sacrificed scientific breadth and diversity for unilateralism. Hell, it's easy to reach consensus if you kick out everyone who disagrees with you.

In yet another example of their bias towards climate destruction, the IPCC, just before they released their fifth report (AR5) in 2013, abandoned the original idea that all scenarios were equally plausible and decided that "business-as-usual" should be attached to one of their most extreme scenarios: Representative Concentration Pathway, RCP 8.5. They abandoned their previous stance of equal-possibility-scenarios and picked a worst-case-scenario as their headline story. As Forbes writer Roger Pielke stated: "The world was no longer heading for a wide range of possible futures, conditioned on enormous uncertainties, but instead was heading with some certainty toward a future characterized by an extreme level of carbon dioxide emissions...The apocalypse has been scheduled."[33]

Why?

Let the speculation begin. Since the IPCC is comprised of international government analysts who are, by nature, political appointees, they are subject to the usual pressures of their government's leanings. For example, if a government in power wants its jobs program to be justified, then they will undoubtedly lean on their analysts to produce results they want. This bias even trickled down into the climate scientists who contributed to the IPCC reports.

In a recent *Forbes* article, Australian Climate Scientist Tom Wigley said: "I'm reminded of what [late Stanford University climate scientist] Steve Schneider used to say. He used to say that as a scientist, we shouldn't really be concerned about the way we slant things in communicating with people out on the street who might need a little push in a certain direction to realize that this is a serious problem. Steve didn't have any qualms about speaking in that biased way. I don't quite agree with that."

The mainstream climate media carried the climate death torch forward. In 2019, Columbia University, one of our nation's most prestigious journalism schools, wrote a story about the problems with climate emergency journalism. In the article, they said: "To avoid climate change catastrophe...the news industry must also transform," and then they wrote a blueprint for how climate panic should be communicated. "So urgent is the challenge...almost nothing else matters in comparison. Journalists need to remember their Paul Revere responsibilities—to awaken, inform, and rouse the people to action."[34]

Continuing, they said: "Moving ahead, climate change would be referred to exclusively as the 'climate emergency, crisis, or breakdown.' Similarly, global warming would be referred to as 'global heating,' and 'climate sceptic' would be replaced by 'climate science denier.'"

The apocalypse has been scheduled, and the blueprint to communicate it has been written.

So let it be written, so let it be done.

Our regular language wasn't enough, so we weaponized it. A snowstorm is now a polar vortex. City planning computer graphics is now climate analog mapping. Poverty is now climate justice. Government-sponsored jobs program? Now it's the Green New Deal. A skeptic is now a climate science denier.

While politicians, their constituents, the IPCC, and the mainstream climate media are all powerful tools in the climate psyence arsenal, perhaps the most powerful of all is the use of selective math to reinforce partisan arguments. *Climaccounting* is a way to selectively use real numbers to reinforce climate arguments, even if the numbers are misleading or downright incorrect. Using it is art as much as science, and the overall point is to cherry pick data in order to support an argument and make it sound 'mathy.' If something has numbers in it, it must be true, right?

Well, no. Fake math is still fake. But one of the amazing things about *climaccounting* is that by showing numbers, it gives it some perceived gravitas—and is therefore prone to being promulgated in the media. Let's illustrate with an example.

In 2019, the International Monetary (IMF) issued a report discussing fossil fuel subsidies, saying that the fossil fuel industry got a whopping $5.2 trillion in 2017 subsidies, or roughly 6.4% of global Gross Domestic Product.[35] *Rolling Stone* picked up the article and added "The United States has spent more subsidizing fossil fuels in recent years than it has on defense spending." Those are *holy-shit-that's-a-lot* numbers, right? Well yes, they would be—if they were true.

Which brings us to a tried-and-true *climaccounting* trick: if you don't like the numbers, just change what you count in that bucket to fit your narrative. The reality, as shown in the report, is that fossil fuel subsidies totaled about $424 billion globally, which is about 1/12 of what was reported. But that didn't sound scary enough, so they simply changed the definition of subsidy. The IMF took all of the air pollution costs and then attributed those generically to "fossil fuels" and called them subsidies. Then, they repeated this process with several additional unaccounted-for external costs and lumped them all into a "subsidy" bucket. The end numbers sound truly ominous. But they are not subsidies and comparing these IMF subsidies to other real subsidies is an incorrect and misleading comparison.

As economist Bjorn Lomborg points out in his *Forbes* article critiquing the IMF's numbers: "The IMF's politically motivated report distracts from the important issue of encouraging the world to dismantle the $424 billion left in fossil fuel subsidies."[36]

Want more instances of *climaccounting* magic? Jobs.

In 2020, the Business Council for Sustainable Energy (BCSE) put out their annual report describing the state of the 2020 sustainable energy. Jobs were included in the report, and the image below circulated that solar energy jobs now eclipsed oil and gas jobs. Clean energy pundits jumped onto this with the theme: "You see? Solar is a bigger job creator than oil and gas!" And certainly, this graph shows that, doesn't it?[37]

U.S. energy overview: Jobs in electricity generation

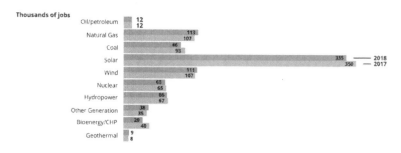

Figure 5 – Jobs in Electricity Generation

Well, no. Notice the qualifier of "electricity generation" and hold that thought for a moment.

In 2017, Allan Hoffman, a former Department of Energy employee, published an article that says: "If a primary national goal is to create jobs in the energy sector, investing in renewable energy is considerably more effective than investing in fossil fuels." Hoffman then proceeded to quote job numbers from The Solar Foundation, a non-profit organization that tracks solar-related employment.

What Hoffman calls "solar employees," The Solar Foundation defines as workers that "support" the solar industry, including lawyers, lobbyists, public relations professionals, government employees overseeing the solar power industry, permits officers, plumbers, electricians, salesmen, land acquisition specialists, and financiers. For solar, all those job functions were included as solar employment, yet for natural gas the functions were limited to "workers directly employed in natural gas extraction." Not only did they not include the same job functions that were included with solar, they omitted other important jobs like construction workers who build the plants, surveyors, equipment builders, and other supporting jobs. The definition of what constitutes a job was expanded and hugely inclusive for solar and was reduced and highly exclusive for natural gas.[38]

Another way to manipulate the job numbers is to be very specific about a market segment function, as in the above "electricity generation" example. Solar is used only for electricity generation, while oil and gas are used in countless other industries. In 2015, oil and gas accounted for over 1.4 million U.S. jobs, compared to 260 thousand in solar. But if you limit the jobs to one particular segment—in this case electricity generation— you can also control the comparison. By intentionally manipulating jobs data, you can come to whatever conclusion you want; but it's like saying a large pepperoni pizza is a vegetable because the sauce contains tomatoes. It's completely misleading.

Moving on, if you peel back the numbers, you find that of the 330 thousand jobs in solar, 150 thousand of them are in California, which leaves 180 thousand spread out across the remaining 49 states. That's 3.7 thousand solar jobs per non-California state, on average. As a comparison, in 2018 there were 3.8 million fast food U.S. jobs, or 76 thousand fast food jobs per state. Is solar really a hot job engine? You can decide for yourself once you're presented with comparative numbers.

Lastly, if you decrease jobs in one sector and replace them in another sector, is that really net job creation or simply job reallocation? Are the 330 thousand solar jobs for electricity generation completely new jobs, or are many of them simply reallocated from a shrinking gas-electricity-generation market slice? It could simply be moving jobs from one segment to another, shuffling the pieces into different sections of the same job board.

Creative accounting, wrongful attribution, guesses-taken-as-givens, incomplete data, inadequate comparisons, selective omissions—all of these are part of the *climaccounting* arsenal. Do we even know what the real numbers are anymore?

~~~~~~~~~~

Before we leave this, perhaps you're wondering: What are the results of these campaigns?

Panic and money, though not necessarily in that order.

Once again let's look to Mr. Gore for guidance. After the success of *An Inconvenient Truth*, Mr. Gore cofounded and is now the Chairman of Generation Investment Management LLP, a fund that invests in sustainability-focused initiatives. As of 9/30/2020, the fund had over $18B of assets under its control. Climate panic is, apparently, big business. And if you can be the one who "identified" the problem, then I have no issue with you being the one to solve it. Fine, more power to Mr. Gore and his church.

But when the church devours its own children, that's when we have to draw the line. As it stands, the main output of decades of climate doom and gloom is fear, primarily our children. We even invented a new term for it: eco-anxiety.

Eco-anxiety is a real thing, and it has real consequences. A recent Washington Post-Kaiser Family Foundation poll of American teenagers showed that 57% said climate change made them feel scared and 52% said it made them feel angry, both higher rates than among adults. Just 29% of teens said they were optimistic.[39] In 2017, the American Psychological Association diagnosed rising eco-anxiety and called it "a chronic fear of environmental doom." Studies from around the world document growing anxiety and depression, particularly among children, about climate change.[40]

Remember Ms. Greta Thunberg from our earlier discussion?

Greta is an amazing girl. Imagine any teenager with enough passion, determination, drive, and gall to step onto a world stage and look adults straight in the eye and tell us to change. Wow, that takes guts. I admire her every time she stands up and talks.

I also get a tear in my eye every time she speaks, because as a parent I can see how much pain she is in. She's hurting, and that pain has turned into helplessness—a feeling so extreme that she feels she has no choice but to yell at us adults to fix things. She's not doing this because she's comfortable, or because she's an "advocate", she's doing it because she hurts. Greta Thunberg is in a tremendous amount of pain, and she's expressing it on a world stage. Imagine how much pain it would take for your child to stand up and yell at adults. It must be excruciating.

How did Greta get into such pain? We did it to her. We adults hurt Greta. And we hurt her so much that she has to travel the world screaming at us.

Greta Thunberg is not a scientist; she offers no new opinions on what's happening with climate change. She is simply parroting to us what we've been telling her and the entire world for years: the world is dying, mankind is the cause, we all have to reverse everything we're all doing or else we're going to die, die, die. This is what she's heard from *us*. We've offered no solutions. Climate deathers yell at climate deniers, the Himalayas are melting, we have 12 years to live. The BBC published an article that month that said that the 12 years is really 11 months. *Eleven months*. Greta Thunberg thought she wouldn't live to see her next summer because of climate change. No wonder she's in such a panic.

Shame on us. How did we let that happen? Never in my life have I seen a situation where adults want to hurt children like this. Not only are we hurting them, we're also celebrating their pain. We scare them to death, then bring in the CNN cameras when the tears start flowing and broadcast their pain to the entire world. It's disgusting.

Greta doesn't understand that her cell phone, her computer, her clothes, her food, the sailboat she traversed the Atlantic in, the lights in her hotel room, the electricity that powered her microphone, the cars, and other modes of transportation she used to get to the United Nations—virtually everything in every step of her life—all used fossil fuels to create and enable her journey. Instead, she just demonizes oil companies because we told her to.

When CNN reports on Islamic terrorists using children as bullet-shields, we gasp in horror. But somehow when we use children as climate-shields we instead hold her up as a hero. What's wrong with this picture?

While Greta and children worldwide continue to suffer, the effects of climate panic continue to appear. In October 2019, an activist with Extinction Rebellion[41] and a videographer were assaulted in a London Tube station by angry commuters. As if that wasn't bad enough, an XR cofounder doubled down in an interview with The Independent and said that genocide like the Holocaust was "happening again, on a far greater scale, and in plain sight" from climate change.[42]

In 2016, *The Nation* published an article entitled "How Do You Decide to Have a Baby When Climate Change Is Remaking Life on Earth?"[43] In 2019, The National Post published an article entitled "Is it Immoral to Have Babies in the Era of Climate Change?"[44] In a 2016 NPR article entitled "Should We Be Having Kids in the Era of Climate Change?" Professor Travis Rieder said: "Here's a provocative thought: Maybe we should protect our kids by not having them."[45]

These are the consequences of decades of climate panic.

Let's celebrate Greta Thunberg for the amazing girl she is, not for the climate-panic we've stuffed into her. We need to stop the global climate terrorism movement now, and come back to a pragmatic, responsible approach to tackle this problem.

CHAPTER 5
MODEL RESULTS, AND THE RISE OF ATTRIBUTION SCIENCE

You've now populated your computer model with some real science, dozens of estimates and assumed variables, and are now ready to hit "Enter." And here is where it gets really fun.

In an earlier chapter we talked about some of the factors that went into the climate models—like temperatures, CO_2 levels, GDP and others—but there are also some basic assumptions that go into interpreting the model results. First, there's an assumption that rising CO_2 is, by its very nature, bad, and that only terrible things will happen as CO_2 levels rise. Second, there's an assumption that increasing temperatures are also fundamentally bad. But are those assumptions valid? Let's discuss them in more detail.

First of all, is CO_2 a pollutant? According to science, no. The world naturally produces gigatons of CO_2. It is a by-product of many natural functions. For example, we emit CO_2 when we breathe. CO_2 is plant food and without it, nothing exists (more on this later). But politically, it's a different story.

Back in 2009, Obama's Environmental Protection Agency (EPA) created the Clean Air Act, under which it attempted to define and regulate a general category of "air pollutants." The

Clean Air Act sought to regulate air pollutants, but first had to define what that phrase meant, and so had to publish a list of official air pollutants. The EPA Administrator's broad definition of air pollutants was the "emissions of which, in his judgment, cause or contribute to air pollution which may reasonably be anticipated to endanger public health or welfare." The EPA's charter is to regulate air pollutants and things that can reasonably affect the public health or welfare.

Still with me? Keep reading.

Enter "Massachusetts vs. The Environmental Protection Agency", a 2007 court case in which the U.S. Supreme Court decided that the Clean Air Act gave the EPA the authority to regulate tailpipe emissions of greenhouse gases. Greenhouse gases, yes, but not specifically CO_2.

But wait, we're still not there.

In 2009, 2 years after the Supreme Court ruling, the EPA issued an "endangerment finding" that said: "The Administrator finds that the current and projected concentrations of the six key well-mixed greenhouse gases—carbon dioxide (CO_2), methane (CH_4), nitrous oxide (N_2O), hydrofluorocarbons (HFCs), perfluorocarbons (PFCs), and sulfur hexafluoride (SF_6)—in the atmosphere threaten the public health and welfare of current and future generations." The finding further said that "these well-mixed greenhouses gases…contribute to the greenhouse gas pollution which threatens public health and welfare."[46]

In other words: the EPA said that "6 key well-mixed greenhouse gases," including CO_2, contribute to public harm. Therefore, they determined that these gases can be considered air pollutants and thus regulated within its charter.

Whew. I'm exhausted.

Back to the beginning question: Is CO_2 a pollutant? No, if you talk to a scientist. Yes, if you talk to a politician or lawyer.

Remember the Science-O-Meter we invented earlier? On a scale of 0 to 10, the science of CO_2 being a pollutant is a 0. (Actually, it would be a negative, but we didn't allow for negative numbers in our makeshift thermometer).

Now the second question: Is rising CO_2 bad?

No. And yes.

Because CO_2 is a natural by-product of human existence and exists naturally in the atmosphere, CO_2 by itself is not a bad thing. In fact, CO_2 is literally plant food: plants need CO_2 to exist. If there was no CO_2 at all in the atmosphere, then there would be no more plants, and if there were no more plants then they would be no human humans (or animals, or anything else that needs oxygen). Scientifically this is known as the Carbon Cycle and is the way the earth regulates itself; without CO_2 there is no life.

Doesn't sound bad so far, does it?

We also know that more CO_2 means more plant life, which typically means more prosperity. We already know that higher levels of CO_2 can increase agriculture at higher elevations and increase vegetation growth. According to the CO_2 Coalition, "At CO_2 levels less than 150 ppm (parts per million), most plants stop growing. Over most of the history of multicellular life on earth, CO_2 levels have been three or four times higher than present levels. Current CO_2 levels of 400 ppm are still much less than optimum for most plant growth."[47]

Still not so bad, is it? Sounds like something we need lots of…which, we do. The problem happens when the Carbon Cycle is out of balance; when there is too much CO_2 in the atmosphere that can be absorbed through natural or artificial means. Mankind emits CO_2 artificially through cars and factories and other means, which adds to the CO_2 count in the atmosphere, and since there aren't enough carbon sinks to offset that rising CO_2, the additional CO_2 begins to act as a magnifying glass and heat blanket. This is known as the Greenhouse Effect. But at what point does all of that additional CO_2 become dangerous and unhealthy?

Well, we don't really know. Again, we rely on computer models. One such study found that,

> If we limit cumulative CO_2 emissions from 2000-2050 to 1,000 Gt (approximately an 80% cut in global emissions), there is a 25% probability of warming exceeding the 2°C limit, and 1,440 Gt CO_2 over that period (an 80% cut in developed country emissions) yields a 50% chance of 2°C warming by the year 2100. If we maintain current emissions levels, there is an approximately 67% chance that we will exceed 2°C warming by 2100.[48]

There you have it. After all is said and done, we need a probability number to answer the question whether or not CO_2 is bad.

Got it? Good. That makes one of us.

Moving on to the second assumption: Are rising temperatures automatically bad? The IPCC reports—and all of the climate reporting—tell us that if temperatures rise by more than 1.5°C bad things will happen. In earlier chapters I illustrated how this basic assumption has been overblown and hystericized by the mainstream climate press, and we've seen the psychological repercussions of some of those over-hyped extremes.

Of course, there is no history that shows these worst-case-scenarios will happen, and we've already seen that there's no real science to prove it. In fact, history shows us the opposite: humanity can flourish with a temperature rise of 1.0°C.

Remember the temperature graph I showed a couple chapters earlier? Here it is again[49] for further discussion.

Global average temperature change

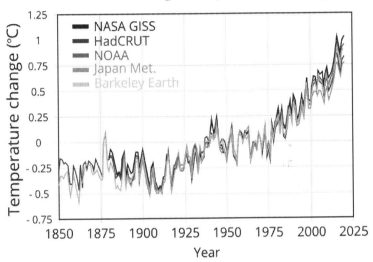

Figure 6. 20th Century Temperature Rise

As the graph shows, from 1900 to 2000 the world warmed by approximately 1.00 C, and no, humanity didn't die. In fact, humanity did quite well during this time. Here are some statistics:

- U.S. Population grew from ~110M to 270M.
- We developed vaccines for and virtually eliminated smallpox, typhoid, cholera, the plague, diphtheria, as well as dozens of others.
- We invented airplanes, televisions, radios, computers, phones, rockets, and the internet.
- Decreased global death rate from 17.2/1000 population to 7.99/1000 population.

- Grew agricultural crop yields across the world by nearly 3 times; corn production in the United States by over 7-fold.[50]

Does that look like a world dying from temperature change? Nope, it doesn't to me either. Looks like a world that's prospering quite well, thank you very much.

As economist Bjorn Lomborg point out: "cold deaths vastly outnumber heat deaths" and that while higher temperatures are now responsible for 100,000 deaths per year, "On average, it has avoided upwards of twice as many deaths, resulting in perhaps 200,000 fewer cold deaths each year."[51]

Why do the model outputs assume it will all be bad? Maybe the answer lies somewhere in Climate Science Attribution.

~~~~~~~~~~

Webster's Dictionary defines attribution as "something, such as a quality or characteristic, that is related to a particular possessor." *The Collins Thesaurus of the English Language* has another word for attribution: blame.

The fundamental idea behind Climate Science Attribution is to find what—and ultimately whom—to blame for climate change. The idea here is to link what is happening with our climate to as many events as possible and then, ultimately, to as many culprits as possible. Of course, wherever there blame is assigned, there are repercussions, and those repercussions usually end up as money. Climate Science Attribution is, quite literally, the method with which to assign companies and people blame and get them to pay for climate solutions. On our Science-O-Meter, Climate Science Attribution rates a 0.

As we showed earlier, President Obama spearheaded the climate blaming framework back in 2007, when the Supreme

Court heard "Massachusetts vs. The Environmental Protection Agency" and gave the EPA the power to regulate six well-mixed greenhouse gases (of which CO_2 was one). Not to be outdone, Columbia University, the creator of the aforementioned how-to-communicate-climate-death blueprint, enlisted their Sabin Center for Climate Change Law to formalize the process of climate blaming.

As their website climateattribution.org states: "Climate attribution science plays a central role in climate litigation and policy-making. The science is central to legal debates on the causal links between human activities, global climate change, and impacts on human and natural systems." These activities are then broken down into 4 thematic elements:

- Climate Change Attribution: Examining how rising concentrations of heat-trapping gases in the atmosphere affect other aspects of the global climate system, such as global mean temperature, sea level, and sea ice.
- Extreme Event Attribution: Examining how changes in the global climate system affect the probability and characteristics of extreme events.
- Impact Attribution: Examining how changes in the global climate system affect humans and ecosystems.
- Source Attribution: Identifying the relative contributions of different sectors, activities, and entities to climate change."[52]

While most areas of so-called climate science attempt to further understanding of climate change, the goal of climate attribution science is to support litigation. Columbia University's legal blueprint entitled, "The Law and Science of Climate Change Attribution," confirms this:

Attribution science is central to the recent climate litigation, as it informs discussions of responsibility for climate change. Indeed, detection and attribution science has long been central to climate litigation…researchers have been developing methodologies to link harmful impacts that were caused or exacerbated by climate change to specific emitters, with an eye towards holding emitters and other responsible parties accountable in court for their contribution to the harms.[53]

The legal framework of climate attribution was first used in 1986 by New York City and Los Angeles to challenge the National Transportation Safety Board's average fuel economy standard, then continued up through 2019 by Ktunaxa Nation to challenge the U.S. Fish and Wildlife Service on mining permits. Of course, it's been used as the main weapon against Big Oil, most notably Exxon-Mobile.

And yet, climate blaming has failed across the board, both in legal and logical constructs. Michael Gerrard, Director of Columbia's Sabin Center for Climate Change Law, acknowledged this in a recent interview:

So far, there's been no success in any of the lawsuits that have tried to make fossil fuel companies or motor vehicle manufacturers or others liable for climate change. A further level of attribution that some are seeking is to say that particular companies are responsible for a certain percentage of greenhouse gas emissions. That has not succeeded anywhere. That's a very, very challenging prospect, particularly since we all know that *climate change is the result of the cumulative emissions of millions of emitting sources over more than a century* [emphasis added]. And so attributing climate impacts to particular companies is very difficult.[54]

Let's say it again, for clarity:

"Climate change is the result of the cumulative emissions of millions of emitting sources over more than a century." That's from the guy who runs The Center trying to hunt down and sue egregious CO_2 emitters.

There isn't a drop of science in there, folks; this is all lawyers.

These days climate attribution has run amok. I call it the Climate Change Attribution Train: we keep adding boxcars in the hope that they actually belong on the train in the first place. And if so, then we hand the bill to somebody. As of this writing, I have seen articles attributing the following to manmade climate change: bad grades, poverty, racial imbalance, fat horses, retreating shorelines, shrinking sheep, birds laying their eggs early, 160,000 deaths/year, 300,000 deaths/year, 360,000 deaths per year, Boy Scout tornado deaths, animal bites, stress, post-traumatic stress…well, you get the picture. Of course, every natural disaster gets somehow linked to climate change; every wildfire, hurricane, rainstorm, heat wave, and cold wave; it's all manmade climate change's fault.

The Climate Change Attribution Train's leaving the station, folks— next stop, MoneyTown. All abooooooooooard! Toot toot!

CHAPTER 6
THE TWIN TOWERS OF FALSE HOPE: NET ZERO AND EMISSIONS REDUCTION

If "COVID pandemic" was the most used phrase in 2020, "net zero" was probably a close second. Net zero (or carbon neutral) refers to achieving a net zero carbon emissions by balancing whatever you release with other forms of savings. The key word here is "net," think of it as breaking even: whatever carbon you emit, you capture or offset by that same amount. [55] A manufacturer who emits 10 tons of CO_2 into the air per month but also sequesters or offsets 10 tons of CO_2 per month would be considered net zero. (Zero carbon refers to the case where no carbon is emitted at all from the onset, while carbon negative, or negative emissions, refers to actually removing more of the carbon you've emitted over time.)

These days it seems everyone has a net zero energy goal. In 2017, New York declared its intentions to be carbon neutral by 2050. Ann Arbor, Michigan, aims to be carbon neutral by 2030. San Francisco aims to be carbon neutral by 2021 (last year!), while California as a whole has a state-wide goal of being carbon neutral by 2045. New York, Hawaii, Massachusetts, and many other states have adopted carbon neutral goals as well.

Companies and organizations have picked up on this, too. Xcel Energy in Colorado is aiming for zero carbon electricity by 2050, and Colorado College recently celebrated its carbon neutrality in 2020. The website Carbon Intelligence lists 92 major corporations that have carbon neutral goals, including British Airways, IKEA, Astra Zeneca, BP, Apple, and Facebook.[56] Joe Biden's 2021 Climate Policy says that the U.S. is committed to zero emissions by 2050. Awesome, right? We'll avert climate destruction in no time, won't we?

Well, no.

Doesn't the IPCC tell us that we need to do something amazingly drastic by 2030 or the earth will reach a tipping point? That means we need to reduce our carbon footprint by enough to keep our temperatures below 1.5°C. That means we not only have to go carbon neutral now, *but also remove megatons of carbon. We have to be carbon negative and actually lower total CO_2 levels. By 2030.*

What good are carbon neutral by 2050 goals?

Not much. Net zero means that our goal is to eliminate the growth of the problem we're creating. We are simply committing to not making things worse. We won't make things better; we just promise to not make it worse. If we commit to net zero in 5 years, for example, it means that we'll emit 5 more years of CO_2 before we level out. In the end, CO_2 emissions will remain 5 years higher.

Back to our publicly stated carbon neutral goals. Companies and governments are committing to not make things worse, and they're going to take 30 to 50 years and countless billions to get there. Is that really a commitment? Hell no. Want to see a real commitment? Look at Microsoft. Not only is Microsoft committed to carbon neutral by 2030, but they're also going to remove all carbon they've emitted since 1975. Now *that* is a commitment. How they'll get there remains to be seen, but that's a real goal that shows they're committed to making things better, not just slowing down the progression of getting worse. Carbon neutral, on the other hand, is a commitment to not making things worse. Seems hardly worth the trouble.

Carbon neutral is a commitment to not making things worse, over decades. Seems hardly worth the trouble.

Joined at the hip with net zero commitments is the concept of future CO_2 emission reductions, another staple of most climate plans. The idea of future emissions reduction is that we take credit today for deploying comparatively cleaner forms of energy and bank the so-called CO_2 savings. As I'll describe in the next pages, future emissions reduction is like a CO_2 promissory note with a variable interest rate, no end date and no payback required. Maybe the best way to discuss the concept of future emissions reduction is through the following analogy.

Imagine going to a doctor and having this conversation:

"You're severely overweight, and if you don't lose 50 pounds now, you'll become very sick," he says.

"Ok, Doctor, I've got a plan for how to lose weight," you say.

"Great! How are you going to do it?" he asks.

"Well, I'm going to the bakery, count up all the cakes, then NOT eat them. Each cake has about 2000 calories, so if I avoid eating 88 cakes then that's what I need to lose 50 pounds. I'll take credit today for not eating those cakes in the future. Voila, I'm skinny!"

Your doctor says, "Well, that's great for not getting fatter, but you still need to lose the 50 pounds."

Thud.

Not a very good diet plan, is it? It's not a very good climate plan either.

Most of our proposed climate solutions call for reducing our global CO_2 emissions over a period of time, with the goal of getting to net zero. Whenever you look at a cleaner energy alternative, for example, they will typically say something akin to "saving 3.5 Giga-tons of carbon emissions," and then they will account for those savings as if they've already happened. But think about what that really means.

First, carbon emission reductions are promises of potential future savings based on dozens of variables. If you replace capacity at a coal plant with a solar farm, for example, the potential future savings of that solar system will be accounted for compared to a coal plant. But what if the energy solar replaces is from a natural gas plant? Since a natural gas plant has lower CO_2 emissions than a coal plant, the potential CO_2 saved by replacing it with solar is lower.

Here on California's central coast, where we get our power from Diablo Canyon's nuclear facility, replacing nuclear capacity with solar capacity will actually increase CO_2 emissions, because nuclear has a lower CO_2 emission footprint than solar. In this particular case, installing solar is actually increasing CO_2 emissions. The point is that emissions reduction accounting is only as good as what it's being compared to and will vary depending on the source it's replacing.

Second, if you displace coal or gas plant capacity with something renewable like solar or wind, the renewable's actual generation will vary over time and by location. We already know about intermittency (how solar and wind resources only produce energy during certain parts of the day), so the amount of energy generated by these sources will fall within a range, and fluctuations of 15-30% in actual energy produced are not uncommon. The amount of energy produced fluctuates daily, which means that the amount of CO_2 they supposedly replace fluctuates daily. Geography plays a significant role as well, as a solar system in Wisconsin will produce different amounts of electricity than the same solar capacity in California.

Third, whenever this accounting occurs, there is not real replacement happening. When you install a solar system and it supposedly replaces a coal system, the coal system is not replaced; rather, the new solar capacity is added, and the overall generation CO_2 footprint is increased. Yes, if entire coal or gas plants are completely decommissioned then solar or wind technically replaces them, but this rarely happens (and if it does, then storage capacity needs to be added to bring it up to 24/7 reliable status). In the end, there is really no actual replacement of energy by the so-called accounting. All we've done is just move the numbers around, like a CO_2 shell game.

Fourth, how do we know that the savings are ever achieved? Renewable energy systems are not audited for their CO_2 reductions, so a running CO_2 scorecard is never kept. We don't really know if CO_2 savings we account for today ever really happen at all.

Climate modelers account for these variables by taking averages and applying them across the board. A wind system's performance in Texas is averaged with a similar system's performance in Ohio, then compared against coal plant averages across a range of power plants. But we never know if the numbers are real or not.

The same logic holds true for electric vehicles and their emissions replacement. A recent *Wall Street Journal* article compared the lifetime emissions of a gas vehicle and a Tesla EV, and noted: "At 20,600 miles, the greenhouse gas emissions from building and driving the two cars are roughly the same" and "emissions will vary based on where the Tesla is charged." If the Tesla charges in a coal-powered utility area, then its emissions replacement will be higher than if at a solar-powered facility.[57]

All of these future numbers are simply estimates, and there's no real way to determine if they're real or not. Contrast those with things that occur in the past that can be measured with real data, and you understand that these are unfair comparisons: past performance is fact, and future performances are unreliable estimates. Imagine using this type of reverse logic in your regular life.

Back to our diet analogy, did you get skinny by not eating 88 cakes? Of course not. You just stopped yourself from gaining weight. You didn't actually save anything. You can't "not-eat-88-donuts" your way to slimness.

Can you pay for your child's college with 50% off coupons from a local grocery store? Did your bank account get bigger? Of course not. In fact, your bank account got smaller, because you had to spend a dollar to save fifty cents. I'm pretty sure you can't pay for Stanford tuition with Vons coupons.

Do you get credit for your dog biting only 1 person instead of the 5 you thought he was going to bite? Does that mean your Akita is a net-4-human-non-biter?

Would a bank loan me more money for a higher-paying job that I don't yet have? "But Sir, I'll be making $75,000 more salary in 5 years, so why can't you give me more money today?" It's almost laughable to think about, isn't it?

Yet that's exactly what we're doing with future-guessing climate math. The logic fails in our everyday lives with everyday things, yet we rely on this faulty thought process almost exclusively when we talk about the climate. We have allowed the potential of future emission savings to somehow be equal to actual, realized savings, and we treat them the same. They are not. Allowing them to be such lulls us into a false sense of security.

All energy systems and vehicles add CO_2 into the atmosphere and will never be CO_2 reducers. Ever. It's not their fault, they're not built to remove CO_2. But taking credit for them not being worse emitters is not solving our climate problem. And pretending they're the same stops us from making real climate progress.

Donut, anyone?

CHAPTER 7
CLIMATE MYTHS

In this chapter I try and shine a light on what I perceive to be the myths permeating our climate discussion. There are certainly more discussion points, but these are the most visible and relevant.

Myth 1: Renewables Can Save the Planet.

I keep seeing this everywhere: "If we go 100% renewables around the world, we can solve all our climate problems." Never mind the morality of rich nations imposing unreliable, intermittent renewable energy on poor nations (and thus preventing their growth), this narrative continues to exist.

Solar often gets touted as the global energy source that's most abundant (enough sunlight hits the earth continually to power the entire earth 10,000 times over), so let's calculate the math to see how it could work out.

First, let's start with the world's anticipated energy usage by 2050. By multiple accounts, it's expected that our global energy needs will be around 199 trillion kilowatt-hours by 2050; to make the math easier, let's just assume 200 trillion kW-hours. If you assume an 8-hour solar day (some people assume more, some assume less), that gets us to 25 trillion watts. We need to manufacture and deploy 25 terrawatts (TW) of solar in order to be 100% solar by 2050. Fine, that's our starting point.

Second, let's subtract from that the amount of installed solar. By the end of 2020, it was estimated that we would have 750 gigawatts of solar installed around the world. If we subtract that from our overall goal we get just under 25 TW.

Third, let's count global solar manufacturing capacity. In 2018, global solar manufacturing was about 116 gigawatts, so by the end of 2020 we can assume it will be about 140 GW of production.

Now we know how much will be needed and how much we can manufacture. Divide one by the other and we'll know the answer. Ready to hit enter? (For full calculations, please refer to this footnote[58]).

If we wanted to have a 100% solar energy world by 2050, we would need to produce 178.56 times more than our current global capacity; and since solar only works 1/3 of the time, we would need to add other energy sources to power us the other 16 hours of the day.

The same number for wind? 135 years, at current capacity.

Of course, there are many different ways to shuffle these energy generation types in our real-world energy mix, but this is a reality-check. There's a reason these various technologies haven't become our energy mainstays: they are technically and technology limited, and they always will be. They work when they can, and are not true substitutes for 24/7 reliable service. Adding intermittent resources onto the grid adds all sorts of other grid challenges, all of which have CO_2 and dollar footprints. Above all, these options are so manufacturing-capacity-limited that they are, in the best case, something we can use to fill-in-the-blanks but not rely on for our total energy future.

The idea that all we have to do is deploy massive amounts of existing renewable energy products and we'll save the planet is fiction. It's not even close to being a realistic option.

Myth 2: Big Oil Bad.

Fossil fuels are the enemy. I know this because everyone keeps telling me so. I keep reading about how fossil fuel companies are the world's enemy, and how they are responsible for our world's climate malaise. Last week, I read stories that 20 fossil fuel companies are responsible for over 33% of the world's carbon emissions since 1965. Never mind that these companies produce things the rest of us consume and use (and therefore emit CO_2 from), these gosh-darn companies are ruining our planet. If we could just get rid of these evil oil companies then we could solve all our growing emissions problems.

Let's spend a day in our life without fossil fuels, shall we?

It's 7 a.m., and it's time to get up. How do you know this? It can't be because of your alarm clock because alarm clocks are plastic, and plastics contain petroleum products. And since you don't use fossil fuels, no clocks for you. (Better dust off your sundial!) You reach for your cell phone, but of course there isn't such a thing because cell phone cases and electronics use petroleum to make, and you don't use those things anymore. (Call your neighbors with a tin can and string!) You get up and walk to the bathroom, but you realize that there's no such thing as indoor plumbing anymore, because metal or plastic pipes are made with—you guessed it—petroleum products. You look at that hole in the floor and hope you don't trip.

Did I say hole in the floor? Sorry! There are no floors because tiles and linoleum and modern construction materials are produced with petroleum, so no floors for you either. If you're lucky you were able to cut down a tree and make planks out of it to walk on, but chances are you used those planks to put overhead since we don't have houses anymore. Aren't you jealous of those dudes in caves?

You go to get dressed but your clothes are made from synthetic fabrics that used oil to produce or natural fabrics that used oil to harvest so, will it be the buffalo or elk hide for you today? (Hope your employer is an animal lover!) You go to the kitchen, but you don't have one, nor do you have a refrigerator. Nothing to eat around here except for those roots in the garden and that pigeon on the fencepost. Bon appétit!

You look for the light switch, but you don't have lights. Or electricity. "But wait, I have a whole group of solar panels that can power my house!" you say. No can do, mi amigo, those solar panels were made in factories that use oil, so no solar panels for you. Or batteries. Or any modern form of energy. Stick a water wheel in that river or burn those logs if you want to power anything. Never mind your carbon footprint.

Let's leave personal grooming out of this analogy, shall we?

You get the point. Literally everything we do every day is somehow touched by the petroleum industry. Everything. It is a simple fact of modern life. It is in our cell phones, computers, TVs, iPods, iPads, clothing, food, transportation, makeup, electricity—everything. If you're protesting climate change and tweeting it, yep, you're using your share of fossil fuels. If you're reading this right now, you're using fossil fuels. If you're reading about evil climate-denying Republicans online, yep, you're using fossil fuels. Sorry to burst your bubble. Try to live a day without the benefits of petroleum products and you will live in a cave eating bugs and grass.

Myth 3: Renewables are Green.

Step one of solar module production? Fire up that enormous, gasoline-fueled earthmover and mow down that mountain. Literally.

You start solar module production with a mining operation, churning up the earth to harvest its precious minerals. Those minerals are then loaded with gas-powered tractors into gas-powered vehicles and transported to coal or gas-powered manufacturing plants; those plants are populated by people who drove their (mostly) gas-powered vehicles to the plant. Those manufacturing plants burn gas and/or coal to turn those minerals into solar modules, at which point those solar modules are loaded into other gas-fueled vehicles for transport. Since most modules are made in China, chances are those gas-fueled vehicles will head to the local port, where other gas-fueled loaders will hoist them onto large diesel ships to chug across the ocean. Once that ship reaches its destination, other gas-fueled loaders will move those containers onto others for local transport to their destination.

Once construction of the solar project begins, they will use gas-fueled vehicles to install and deploy the entire system. Notice anything familiar about all that?

Every step of the renewable energy production process is fueled by gas and/or coal and its infrastructure. If the gas or coal industry died tomorrow, it would take the entire renewable energy industry down with it. You literally cannot make one solar module without using gas/coal infrastructure. Not one.

Yes, when you install that solar system onto its destination it will cease to emit any CO_2 at that point—until its 20 years is up and it has to be replaced by the same process we outlined above. Oh, and those old modules will have to be recycled or dumped using gas-fueled infrastructure.

Here's the point: every energy source is a net CO_2 increaser. **Every energy source—no matter if it's called clean or green—emits CO_2 and always adds to the total CO_2 amount in the atmosphere.** Here's the same point, in picture form.[59]

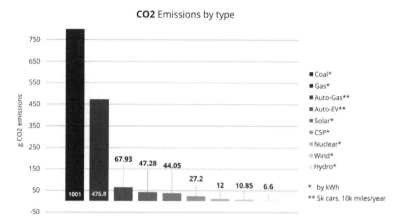

Figure 7. Lifetime CO_2 Emissions (grams), by type

On the far left is coal generation, at 1001 grams of CO_2/kW-hour emitted, while hydro has the lowest CO_2 emissions at 6.6/kW-hour. Electric vehicles emit a bit less than gas vehicles, but the difference isn't as much as many believe. When it's all laid out, the one resounding fact is this: all things that generate electricity/power add CO_2 into the atmosphere. All of them. If you install an energy system—even if it's renewable—you will add CO_2 into the atmosphere.

The bottom line? Renewables are not green; they are simply less brown than alternatives. Beige energy, maybe? Every single renewable system is a net carbon emitter; *they will never be net carbon reducers*. As we'll see in Myth #4, slowing future carbon growth is not the same as lowering carbon today.

Myth 4: Climate science is settled, 97% of scientists agree.

Ah yes, the now-infamous "97% consensus" metric.

First uttered by Mr. Gore in *An Inconvenient Truth*, then memorialized endlessly by the climate media, the idea that climate science is settled (and thereby not open to discussion) and that scientists have reached 97% consensus has been popularized for so long it's an internet meme. Never mind the validity of scientists *voting* on whether or not a piece of science is true or not (doesn't the fact that scientists need to vote on something make it, by definition, *not* science?), this percentage has been repeated ad nauseum in the climate discussion. Talk to any true believer and they will undoubtedly quote this as proof of near-unanimous scientific certainty of our impending climate doom—and also as proof of those anti-voters and their scientific incompetence. The term you'll hear often about those defiant 3% non-voters is "debunked."

Since it's a number that's out there in circulation, it begs the question: Where did it come from? Finding a definition is not easy, but this study[60] sheds some light on the numbers. Scientists in the study examined 11,944 climate science abstracts, looking for either "global climate change" or "global warming." Of those, 66.4% presented no opinion on anthropogenic warming (AGW) and 32.6% expressed one. Of those who expressed an opinion, 97.1% endorsed the *opinion* that humans are causing global warming.

If you step back and do the math, 3,774 out of 11,944 abstracts expressed the opinion that humans cause global warming, which comes to 31.6%. 31.6% is a far cry from 97% consensus, isn't it? It's just more *climaccounting* magic: If you count only the people who had an opinion and omit those who didn't, you can back your way into the 97% consensus number. But presenting it as comprehensive scientific consensus is misleading and just plain nonsense.

Myth 5: Solar is the cheapest form of electricity.

Until it isn't.

This is like standing atop Shaquille O'Neal's shoulders then declaring: "Look at me! I'm the tallest person in the world!" You may feel tall at the moment, but as soon as you jump off his shoulders, you'll be normal size again.

Electricity is much more complicated than that, of course, all the more so because of all the things that solar doesn't have to pay for. Solar systems plug into the electricity grid that's been running for decades; solar pays for its access to the grid but is not burdened with its share of all the other costs. Solar doesn't have to pay for grid availability, the grid operator does; when the sky gets cloudy, the regular grid kicks in and takes over. If the grid goes down completely (as it did in February 2021 in Texas, for example), solar can rightfully say, "It's a grid issue, not ours." Fine. But someone else is paying for reliable electricity, not solar. Solar gets free grid reliability from someone else.

There is also the intermittency issue, which I discussed in previous chapters. Solar works only when the sun is shining and ramps up and down as sunshine ebbs and flows. When it's a perfectly sunny day and the grid is humming along, solar works at its peak and is fantastic for peak shaving. In those ideal circumstances, solar can be the cheapest incremental form of electricity. But what about at midnight? Then, the cost of solar electricity becomes infinite because solar systems are producing no electricity whatsoever. In other words, a billion dollars could not power one lightbulb with solar electricity at midnight, so the "cheapest electricity" claim is meaningless.

Therefore, if you stop counting when you're not generating electricity, your numbers will look awesome; but if you calculate your energy production over all 24 hours then your numbers will be 3-4 times higher. The same thing is true of wind: the $ per kW-hour numbers only apply when wind turbines are spinning.

So, if you're going to compare energy sources, then compare them fairly. Otherwise, it's just more sleight-of-hand climaccounting.

Myth 6: Climate Change is an existential crisis.

An existential crisis is a situation in which your very existence is in danger. So, if climate change is an existential crisis, why are you reading this? Why aren't you packing up your family and all your belongings into a van and driving up into the mountains forever? Why are you continuing to use your phone, the internet, your computer, wearing clothes, eating food, living in manufactured homes, driving anywhere at all—and continuing to consume fossil fuels? Why are you living your lives mostly as normal and not changing everything to save your and your family's lives? Why aren't you saving your own life?

Because climate change isn't an existential crisis. Climate change is like the Doritos you had for lunch: watch it and cut back, but they're not going to kill you. Really. Enough already. Whoever says that it is, feel free to take their Doritos. You have my permission.

Myth 7: Climate Change is racist.

Of all the climate change stories out there, this one may be the most infuriating. Articles about climate change being racist are plentiful, as exemplified by this June 29, 2020, *Washington Post* article entitled "Climate change is also a racial justice problem."[61] The article quotes studies that "Black and Hispanic communities in the U.S. are exposed to far more air pollution than they produce through actions like driving and using electricity. By contrast, white Americans experience better air quality than the national average, even though their activities are the source of most pollutants." This and countless other articles go on and on about how climate change is inherently racist, and they're given provocative names like "climate justice" and "social justice" to be the rallying cries to solve them.

Those who think clearly see this type of appropriation as what it is: a way to get people to pay for climate change pet projects. Politicians and activists/alarmists have known for decades that the quickest path into White Guilter's wallets is by slapping the racist label on something; as of this writing even Pete Buttigieg, the Department of Transportation Secretary under Joe Biden, called roads and highways racist.[62] Really.

So, if the argument goes that people of color are affected most by climate change, then let's play that all the way out. We know that the argument is primarily an economic one: people in poverty and people of color will bear a disproportionate cost for pollution and other things related to climate change. As the article says: "the people most at risk from climate change have the fewest resources to cope." In other words, get people jobs, and their risks from climate change drop dramatically.

We also know that access to cheap, reliable energy is a necessity for thriving economies, jobs, and homes, and that those without access to that energy will be significantly limited in their ability to lead healthier, more productive lives. In fact, access to affordable, reliable energy is absolutely necessary for modern living at even the most basic level.

Enter intermittent, unreliable, expensive clean energy.

If access to cheap and reliable energy is necessary for basic human survival, then limiting access to that energy can be seen as an egregious burden. Replacing cheap, reliable energy with intermittent, unreliable, more expensive energy can even be seen as punitive. If your energy source only works for 1/3 of the time your previous energy source did, then you've cut the access poor people of color have to an energy source by 2/3. Put another way, you have just taken a resource that is required to help lift people of color out of poverty and cut their access to it by 66%.

"But wait," you say, "just add batteries and/or other types of storage in order to fill in that other 2/3." Clean energy goals achieved.

Really? So poor people of color, who already can't afford the clean energy system that's been thrust upon them now need to spend thousands more to make energy they previously got for cheap? We already know they have the fewest resources to cope, so this is doubly punitive. It's not going to happen.

I'll say it differently: Climate panic is inherently racist.

Why? Because climate panic leads to bad policies like an over-proliferation of expensive, intermittent energy. And if people of color are affected by the ravages of climate change, then removing 2/3 of their existing energy supply makes those ravages more significant.

Let's take this argument a step further, into the developing world. Many countries in Africa, for example, have underdeveloped economies and need that same access to cheap, reliable electricity, and many of these countries are primarily Black. If energy access is required to lift them out of poverty, and we're going to limit their access to that energy because of misguided clean energy policies, then we are literally limiting that population's ability to become economically stable. By forcing them to use intermittent, expensive clean energy, we are ensuring their generational poverty, conditions that will primarily affect people of color.

I'll be blunt: ban fossil fuels from undeveloped countries in favor of renewable energy and you guarantee that people of color will remain in poverty. All of this leads me to my first and final conclusion: **Climate panic that leads to hysteria-fueled** policy is racist. If you believe that climate change is racist, then climate panic is doubly so.

CHAPTER 8
SO WHAT NOW?

We've endured decades of onslaught by the climate media that we're all dying, the earth is on its last legs, and fossil fuels are to blame. They've scared our children and promoted hysteria at the expense of true, real, physical, scientific transparency. Celebrities and politicians have warned us that climate change is an existential crisis— while still flying in their private jets—and have set the stage for trillions in spending to help solve it. Columbia University even wrote a blueprint for how climate death should be communicated, to make sure everyone gets it right.

Empirical science has been replaced with future-oriented models without telling anyone. We've taken temperature and CO_2 measurements—which require empirical science to measure and interpret—mixed them with dozens of estimates, assumed economic and social responses to climate factors, and put them all together into computer models that try and predict the future, then hit "Enter." We call it science, although we know, fundamentally, that it's not the type of science that is indisputable; in truth, calling predictive models scientific fact only breeds more confusion. We've fused physical science with scientific theory and created this new form of science-infused rhetoric, which I call psyence. Then we slather our own version of psyence across the world and reject those don't believe it.

Then the lawyers got involved. President Obama took CO_2 to the Supreme Court, whose endangerment finding said that

CO_2 and 5 other mixed-together manmade gases could be considered dangerous and could therefore be regulated by the EPA. Science says CO_2 is beneficial, but now lawyers say it's bad. Columbia University's law school then developed climate-science-attribution legal constructs as a way to start blaming (and collecting from) CO_2 emitters, yet despite unanimous court losses, climate attribution has taken hold. Now we blame fat horses, small sheep, windstorms, hailstorms, rainstorms, wildfires, poverty, racism, and bad grades on manmade climate change. Pay up!

Despite all of this, most of us believe that there is actually a climate problem. We genuinely want to understand the severity of our climate woes and work together to help solve them. Even with all the fluff and bluster, we want to put humanity onto a more sustainable path. So, we have to pick a starting point.

First, global temperatures. Yes, they're rising, and yes slowing them down is important. While some increases in temperatures are beneficial, having them climb unabated is undoubtedly worrisome.

Second, rising CO_2 levels. Given the same constraints as with global temperatures (mainly, questionable methods on looking backwards), we can still show that CO_2 levels are rising.

Third, the causation between the first two: Do rising CO_2 levels raise global temperatures? Well, we don't really know, but there does seem to be some correlation between the two, and shouldn't we pay attention to that link anyway?

Fourth, the prospective catastrophes supposedly caused by both rising temperatures and rising CO_2 levels. What will the effects of these higher temperatures be? Who the hell knows? There's no science that tells us this; it's speculation, pure guesswork. (On our Science-O-Meter, Doomsday scenarios are a 0. Let's not even go there.)

Good? Ok, not perfect of course, but it at least gives us a starting point. Yes, temperatures are rising—check!— CO_2 levels are rising—check!—mankind is having some effect on rising temperatures—check minus!—and we have enough to begin. If we're going to affect global temperatures and we believe CO_2 is the culprit, we have to figure out a way to manage global CO_2. Based on that, our mantra should be: **lower CO_2 levels in order to lower global temperatures—and pay for nothing that doesn't do that quickly.**

Hold that thought.

The IPCC and many of our other energy agencies have shown how different solutions could affect global temperatures, and it's worth showing how it lays out.[63]

Staying Below 2 Degrees of Global Warming

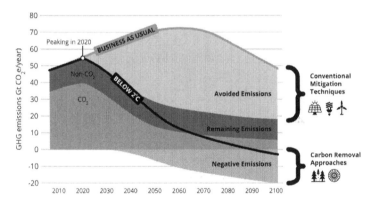

Source: Adapted frm UNEP 2016
For more information, visit wri.org/carbonremoval

WORLD RESOURCES INSTITUTE

Figure 8. Two Degrees of Global Warming.

In this figure, the line represents the desired trajectory of keeping our temperatures below 2°C (the temperatures the IPCC recommends), while the shaded areas show different approaches to achieving this desired trajectory. Conventional mitigation techniques like renewable energy and mass electrification are shown in the gray areas and fall into the category of "avoided emissions." Non-CO_2 emissions, such as livestock and waste, are shown in blue, and show a fairly steady effect all the way around. Carbon removal techniques like reforestation and carbon capture are shown in green and are in the category of "negative emissions."

Whenever I see this graph, I'm always struck a first, inescapable conclusion: we can't "avoided-emissions" our way to climate salvation. Decarbonization is a guaranteed losing strategy. Even if we slow down or completely eliminate our emissions growth, we can never reach our temperature reduction goals. Ever.

The narrative makes logical sense. If the problem is that we have too much CO_2 in the air, and that over-abundant CO_2 is making temperatures rise, then slowing down the growth of its rise will never make it go away; the only thing we're doing is not making it worse. But we still have to contend with all the CO_2 already here, what's called legacy CO_2. We can stop the growth, but legacy CO_2 remains and keeps us from lowering global temperatures.

The second thing that strikes me when I look at this figure is that we need to deploy carbon removal techniques and technologies at-scale to meet our goals; we have to commit to removing excess CO_2 from the atmosphere. Even in this simplistic graph it's the only way we get there. Again, this makes sense: it's not enough to stop the growth of CO_2, we have to reverse it and remove legacy CO_2.

So, what do we solve first?

Project Drawdown[64], a non-profit environmental organization founded in 2014, has attempted to answer that question. They developed a list of potential solutions and their potential emissions impacts, categorized by sectors: food/agriculture, electricity, buildings, land sinks, coastal/ocean sinks, engineered sinks, and health/education. They created 2 scenarios: one for a 2°C temperature rise by 2100, and a second for a 1.5°C rise, then prioritized those items based on the most anticipated emissions savings.

For the 1.5°C scenario, here are some highlights:

- The top 5 recommendations were, in order: reduced food waste, improved health and education, plant-rich diets, refrigerant management, and tropical forest restoration.
- Of the top 20 recommendations, 7 are land sinks, 4 are electricity generation, and 2 are energy efficiency.
- For all solutions, food/agriculture, land use, and land sinks had the most potential savings (444.18 Gigatons), followed by electricity generation (177.8 Gt), industry and industry/buildings (118.96 Gt), and buildings with 70.35 Gt.

For the 2°C scenario, here are some highlights:

- The top recommendations were: onshore wind turbines, utility scale solar production, reduced food waste, plant-rich diets, and improved health and education.
- Of the top 20 recommendations, 11 are land sinks, 4 are electricity generation.
- For all solutions, food/agriculture, land use, and land sinks had the most potential savings (645.9 Gigatons), followed by electricity generation (410.78 Gt), industry and industry/buildings (139.28 Gt), and transportation (97.425 Gt).

What a great starting point. These lists are comprehensive and give a very good summary of the options that could be available. They focus primarily on emissions reduction, which as we've already discussed, has its own limitations. Most of the scenarios include cost information, some of them include potential savings, and some include profit. Unfortunately, many of the top emissions reduction candidates have no cost information, which makes them very difficult to analyze and prioritize. Additional information which would undoubtedly change the rankings are:

1. Cost to increase manufacturing capacity.
2. Time to increase and implement manufacturing capacity.
3. Time to implement and realize benefits from.
4. And last and certainly the most important: What is the expected temperature reduction for each solution?

With the current sorting, 6 of the top 20 emissions reduction candidates have no cost information (for a total of >365 Giga-tons), which make them nearly impossible to plan for and implement. But what happens if we sort the potential solutions by cost to implement? If we do, we get the following rankings:

	Solution	2°C Scenario G-tons	$/ton
1	Peatland Protection and Rewetting	26.03	0 .
2	Indigenous Peoples' Forest Tenure	8.69	0
3	Carpooling	7.7	0
4	Public Transit	7.51	0
5	System of Rice Intensification	2.78	0
6	Nutrient Management	2.34	0
7	Walkable Cities	1.44	0
8	Sustainable Intensification for Smallholders	1.36	0
9	Reduced Food Waste	87.45	No $

10	Health and Education	85.42	No $
11	Plant-Rich Diets	65.01	No $
12	Tropical Forest Restoration	54.45	No $
13	Alternative Refrigerants	43.53	No $
14	Temperate Forest Restoration	19.42	No $
15	Forest Protection	5.52	No $
16	Grassland Protection	3.35	No $
17	Coastal Wetland Protection	0.99	No $
18	Low-Flow Fixtures	0.91	1.63
19	Recycling	5.5	1.8
20	Managed Grazing	16.42	2.04
21	Landfill Methane Capture	2.18	2.7
22	Improved Clean Cookstoves	31.34	4.1
23	Multistrata Agroforestry	11.3	4.78
24	Biogas for Cooking	4.65	5
25	Regenerative Annual Cropping	14.52	5.36
26	Perennial Staple Crops	15.45	5.37
27	Bamboo Production	8.27	6.32
28	Conservation Agriculture	13.4	6.9
29	Silvopasture	26.58	7.4
30	Tree Plantations (on Degraded Land)	22.24	7.5
31	Abandoned Farmland Restoration	12.48	7.87
32	Alternative Cement	7.98	7.9
33	Distributed Solar Photovoltaics	27.98	9.1
34	Tree Intercropping	15.03	9.77
35	Refrigerant Management	57.75	10.9
36	Geothermal Power	6.19	13
37	High-Efficiency Heat Pumps	4.16	18.43
38	Biomass Power	2.52	20.29
39	Onshore Wind Turbines	47.21	21.18
40	Smart Thermostats	6.99	22.03
41	Concentrated Solar Power	18.6	25.5
42	Water Distribution Efficiency	0.66	26.36
43	Bioplastics	0.96	26.5

44	Methane Digesters	9.83	28.1
45	Small Hydropower	1.69	29.21
46	Building Automation Systems	6.47	33.76
47	District Heating	6.28	34.95
48	Utility-Scale Solar Photovoltaics	42.32	36.15
49	Composting	2.14	39.1
50	Insulation	16.97	44.25
51	Improved Rice Production	9.44	49
52	Perennial Biomass Production	4	57.58
53	Offshore Wind Turbines	10.44	60.54
54	Waste-to-Energy	2.04	66
55	Nuclear Power	2.65	72.45
56	Telepresence	1.05	81.9
57	Biochar Production	2.22	87.8
58	Efficient Trucks	4.61	105.4
59	Efficient Ocean Shipping	4.4	120.4
60	LED Lighting	16.07	124.45
61	Efficient Aviation	6.27	133.3
62	Ocean Power	1.38	144.93
63	Farm Irrigation Efficiency	1.13	196.4
64	Solar Hot Water	3.59	200
65	Dynamic Glass	0.29	238
66	Hybrid Cars	7.89	345.5
67	Electric Cars	11.87	377.5
68	Recycled Paper	1.1	413.6
69	High-Speed Rail	1.3	469
70	Micro Wind Turbines	0.09	587
71	Electric Bicycles	1.31	877.8
72	High-Performance Glass	10.04	902
73	Green and Cool Roofs	0.6	1038
74	Bicycle Infrastructure	2.56	2945
75	Electric Trains	0.1	6300

Figure 9. List of Prioritized Solutions

(data from drawdown.org, sorted by calculated $ / ton)

Quite a list, isn't it? This is now a list of climate options, sorted from cheapest-to-highest-to-implement. It's a list of viable options, sorted by best bang for the buck. Now we can compare this list with what's actually being planned for and see which would be the best way to move forward.

Since net zero and emissions reduction keep getting all the press, let's see if those options make good energy policy.

How many energy options are in the top 10 (as in cheapest savings/ton CO_2)?

None.

How many energy options are in the top 20?

None.

How many energy options are in the top 30?

None.

The top energy item is distributed solar at #33, at a cost of $9.1/ton. That means there are 32 items that could be cheaper to implement and would have greater CO_2 reductions than rooftop solar; other energy options are even lower than that.

What about electric vehicles? We're spending trillions to convert the world's transportation infrastructure towards EVs, in the hope that this will reduce enough carbon to save the planet. Surely this is a good spend, isn't it?

In this list, electric vehicles come in at #67, just below Hybrids at #66—and this is out of a total of 75 options. EV spending, as rated by the CO_2 reduction benefits it would receive per dollar spent, is at the bottom of the list of viable options. And yet, we're spending trillions to support this transition. This is a far cry than what's currently being promoted by our political and big climate media advocates.

If we include time-to-implement-and-realize-benefits-from, this list would, of course, change dramatically again. Since we know that electricity decarbonization plans would take decades to realize benefits from, these would undoubtedly drop down in the list, while carbon removal items like natural land sinks would jump to the top. Money will always be an issue, so items that cost trillions and delay results for decades would also drop down dramatically.

Given that, items that lower our CO_2 the quickest and the least expensively and drop temperatures by the most should be given top priority.

There's also a secondary benefit: If we implement CO_2 reduction measures and we don't affect temperatures, then we've proven the relationship between CO_2 and temperatures once and for all. If these don't work, then a massive decarbonization strategy that would slow CO_2 growth over decades will never work to lower temperatures, and we can focus on other things.

CHAPTER 9
A PATH FORWARD

There are no magic bullets when it comes to the climate. After we've sifted through the misinformation and invective, climate change becomes a real problem that requires our direct attention. Unfortunately, the solutions being proposed are incomplete and expensive, based on minimal and incomplete science, and they don't directly attack the problem. Rather than propose a list of direct solutions, I advocate for a process and outlook that could get us there. I advocate for climaturity: a process where we're transparent and open and inclusive about the problems we face and the resources we need to spend. Anything short of that gets us to, well, exactly where we're at today, which is pretty much nowhere. We need a new and sane approach, so let me offer the following ideas (in no particular order).

Let's Agree that Temperature Reduction is the End Game
Our overall goal needs to be temperature reduction, not emissions reduction, or tech proliferation, or jobs, or whatever. We need to start with the things that affect temperature the most. If we don't know the answer, then why bother implementing them? It is a waste of money if we don't. We need to spend money on things that will have the most direct temperature reduction impact.

Carbon Negative First

Decarbonization over a 30-50-year period—while spending trillions in the process—won't get us there. Time is a factor, so we don't have 50 years to wait for progress. As we've already seen, the process and accounting methods we use in future-looking carbon reduction is iffy at best, and we don't have 50 years to find out how wrong we've been. We need to start our carbon negative journey by funding and deploying both technical and natural solutions today.

Implement Natural Solutions First

Plant trees until we figure everything else out. Then keep planting trees even after we do. Carbon removal technology development and deployment will take decades, but we have hundreds of natural solutions available today if we choose to implement them. Do it now.

Adaptation is a Viable Option.

One of the most interesting aspects about our climate modeling process is the idea that humanity will not react at all to whatever happens to our planet. The models assume temperature growth, economic options, energy adoption rates and dozens of other variables, yet assume that we as humans will simply stand idly by as our planet collapses around us.

What a silly notion. Like every species, mankind will adapt to however the world changes. If coastlines rise, we'll build homes further away from them. If mountains melt over decades, we'll relocate onto higher ground. If things get too hot, we'll deploy air conditioning and other ways to survive the heat.

We have been adapting to environmental changes our entire existence. The Netherlands has been underwater since it began and has continued to evolve its water management capabilities. In 2007, Hurricane Katrina killed 1800 people and destroyed much of New Orleans, but we adapted, rebuilt the levee system, and lowered deaths to 150 when Hurricane Ida hit in 2021. We will adapt to how the world changes and should consider it as one of primary options to fight climate change.

Conservation is also a Viable Option

All of our energy scenarios assume that our global energy usage will grow unabated, but what if we were able to slow this down? What if we all used 25% less stuff than we do now? Using less stuff would save trillions and would give our natural systems to catch up. Conservation just makes good sense.

For those who say it can't be done, I'll offer up the year 2020 as Exhibit A. Driven by COVID-fueled conservation, the U.S. dropped our overall emissions by 11%, 15% in transportation. We stayed home, and we used less stuff. We did in 1 year through conservation what nearly 50 years of climate panic couldn't.

Develop and Implement Consistent Climate Accounting

Let's stop the *climaccounting* sleight-of-hand. At this point in our climate evolution, we need real numbers, real facts, and real comparisons. If we penalize one energy source for something, we need to include that factor in all of the comparisons. No cherry picking the data. Call out those who do. We need to compare things fairly. We also need new metrics, those with which we can compare options fairly and evenly. **I propose the following: dollars spent/temperature reduction/time.** We just don't know how much it's going to cost to reverse our temperatures, so we need to change that now. We need to know what our options are.

Implement the Cheapest and Most Cost-Effective Items First

We need to perform cost-benefit analyses on all potential options, with the same standard comparative math we developed in the previous section. Which are the cheapest options to implement in order to get us the quickest benefits? If we don't know, then we don't implement it. Period.

Decarbonize, But Don't Do It Blindly

A massive ramp-up of "electrify everything" will not lead us to climate salvation. We'll spend trillions and never reach our temperature-reduction goals. Yes, it plays well in the climate press, and yes, politicians love it, but it falls short every time. Let's continue our gradual makeover of our electrical and transportation grids with cleaner alternatives, but only where it doesn't break the bank. The world isn't ready for things that will cost us so much and deliver so little after decades.

✳ Challenge the Narrative

Ask questions, challenge what you don't understand. Put people on the spot. Don't let yourself be bullied. Most of what we're being told is not science, it's opinion and/or computer predictions. This is no way to justify spending trillions. We need to call people out on both sides of the aisle on their irrelevant and ridiculous rhetoric.

We Need Bipartisan Support

Let's say this all together now: everything, everything, everything must have support from both Democrats and Republicans. And not just one token vote so it plays well with Corporate Media. I mean real bipartisan support. No more of this 2-years-on, 2-years-off crap, we need things that will truly span administrations. We have to have continuous commitment.

Full Climate Transparency

I call for a 6-12 month public campaign with climate scientists in front of Congress, with full transparency. We need both sides of the aisle being able to ask questions *in public*. We need this out in front of everybody, so we know what the reality is, what the reality isn't, and how much it's all going to cost. Enough of this cloak and dagger/hidden in international meeting minutes nonsense. Make it all public.

Stop the Panic

It's just crazy. There is no way to justify this type of misdirection and overhype. We are doing a huge disservice to everyone by continuing the climapocalypse narrative.

Stop Terrifying Our Children

This is even crazier. Stop telling my children that the world is going to die tomorrow. It's not, so quit saying it.

Make Changes Yourself

No Paris (or Kyoto or Cancun or Glasgow) or any other international agreement is not going to save us. Neither is the Green New Deal or whatever else it's called by the time you read this. It's just not going to happen. If you are a true believer, then change your life to make it happen. Give up fossil fuels completely. Rearrange your life to make it happen. Rearrange your children's lives to make it happen.

Leverage the Capitalist Profit-Motive

Greed is good. Remember when Gordon Gecko, the slick-haired huckster, said that in the movie *Wall Street*? Many cringed. His point? Selfishness will direct people's energies towards making money, which grows businesses, creates employment, creates opportunities, and can cause a tremendous amount of good in the process.

We in solar figured that out years ago. Before subsidies and rebates and other financial incentives came into play, solar was relegated to boats and cabins in the woods. Then financial engineering concepts like Power Purchase Agreements, Investment Tax Credits, and others were designed and showed companies how they could make money; many of you reading this invented those concepts. Once people figured out how to profit it from it there's been double-digit worldwide growth since then. (There wasn't green until there was GR$$N.)

If we collectively figure out how to make money at solving climate change, then selfish profit-making interests could go towards solving our most pressing problems. Imagine all those international resources focused on solving climate change and, oh by the way, they're making a helluva lot of money too. Isn't that a good thing?

Incentivize Changes

Imagine governments paying us to conserve, plant trees, stop driving, or anything else we could individually contribute to help counterbalance what's happening on our planet. Instead of paying billions in subsidies to car companies to make electric vehicles that only the wealthy can afford, how about if those same subsidies incentivized us all—and I mean all—to change our collective behavior towards the common good? Pay us to not drive, pay us to plant greenery in our yards, pay us to carpool. There are thousands of things we can do that wouldn't require the transformation of our entire world's infrastructure to be effective.

EPILOGUE

What's all the Fuss on Planet Gus?
inspired by Dr. Seuss
Written by Yours Truly,
Just Because…

I went down to the store today,
To shop for all of us,
And when I stepped out of my car,
I met a guy named Gus.

I can't help but see, good sir,
Said Gus, as I walked near,
You drove up in your car today,
To get from there to here.

Perhaps you just don't understand,
How close we are to dying,
Our planet is on life support,
Or do you think I'm lying?

Of course I see, I said to Gus,
Our planet's very dear,
I would, of course, walk down the road,
If I lived more than near.

Allow me to enlighten you,
You seem a caring chap,
The auto that you drove to here,
Is really full of crap.

There's steel and bolts and black rub-ber,
All made from precious land,
And certain-ly you know by now,
It's made with bloody hands.

Buy one of these instead, Gus says,
I promise you, it's cleaner,
He turned and pointed to his car,
His EV said it's greener.

But wait, dear Gus, I just don't see,
It's all a bit confusing,
Why is it that *your* steel and bolts,
Are so much less abusing?

Those batt'ries that you have inside,
Are they so clean and pretty?
I know the gas I burn is bad,
But is yours so un-dirty?

I now see what the problem is,
Gus said with eyes afire,
It seems to me that you are one,
Of those we call Denier.

You drive your car and buy your food,
Your kids get ed-u-cation,

Instead of spending hard-earned cash,
On planet devas-tation.

How dare you not pa-nic like me,
Who do you think you are?
Do you think it's silly as,
This putrid little car?

Your food, your shoes, your com-pu-tot,
Your dang-ly pant-a-loons,
Are made with oily, blacky stuff,
We know caus-es monsoons!

Monsoons, you say, that seems ex-treme,
How is that, can you say?
Wea-ther has been 'round, dear Gus,
At least since first of May.

I understand, let's all conserve,
And make some cleaner choices,
But don't you think, let's not just scream,
But find some saner voices?

We've heard the voice, Gus said so loud,
His Highness, Sir Al Gore!
He told us the de-bate is done,
And that we're in a war!

He showed us that we need wind-mills,
And sun — he taught the class!
And when you burn down shrubs and trees,
Just call it biomass.

Your problem, I can see right now,
Is that you don't get science,
Heat and C-O-2, good sir,
Form an ucky-muck al-liance.

C-O-2, not 1 or 3,
Just causes so much trouble,
It heats and speats and mag-ni-vates,
And makes a poison bubble!

You breathe it in, you die right there,
Your living is no longer!
I can't believe we're still alive,
Because it's grown so stronger.

How dare you drive, how dare you eat?
How dare you try to hide?
Your siggly, iggly, piggly life,
Will lead to eco-cide!

You heat and spew and igno-rate,
And con-sume what's not broke,
What's frus-ter-ating most for me,
Is how are you not Woke?

That dirty C-O-2, I say,
It's 2, not 1 or 3,
Isn't that the food we need,
To feed these greeny trees?

They soak it up, they drink it whole,
They swallow it completely,

In fact if Number Two was gone,
Would we be here so neatly?

The more of it, it seems to me,
Makes green and reds grow fatter,
If we be-gone with all of it,
Won't our lives be bad-der?

I'm Woke enough, dear Gus, I say,
Believe me when I feel it,
But if our planet is so broke,
Why can't we just re-tree it?

With dirt and trees and buggy stuff,
All easy to de-ploy,
All that stuff's been working fine,
Since 'fore I was a boy.

Sticks and stones, oh that's just droll,
Gus asked, is that a joke?
On-ly high-tech-nol-o-gy,
Can fix all that is broke.

We need new Blurks and Stid-gels,
And sunny bloppy-tagnants,
I'd try to ex-plain more to you,
But you are so ig-NOR-ant.

Of course we need, to make that stuff,
More people by the gobs,
Washing green is eas-i-er,
If we just call them jobs.

Us Climate Wolk Folk know the way,
With perfect-good distinction,
That giving up our hard-earned cash,
Prevents human ex-tinc-tion!

The only way I see right now,
Our planet to be saved,
Is give up all your worldly goods,
And go to live in caves.

So give me all your shoes 'n stuff,
I'll help you save your fam'ly,
Give me ti-tle to your car,
I'll sell it all on e-Bay.

No need to thank me, I'm the guy,
Who's too above "you're welcome",
Oh, by the way, that cave you're in?
We need that hole's lith-i-um.

FREQUENTLY ASKED QUESTIONS

Following the completion of *Climaturity*, I sat down with my publisher for an interview. What follows is the abridged version of that interview. You can listen to the entire audio interview at **Climaturity.com**

Note to Reader:

This chapter is essential an interview transcription, so please forgive us for any grammatical errors.

Q. You invented the word *Climaturity*. Can you define it?

Climaturity is a call out for a calm, pragmatic and transparent dialog about the climate, which is pretty much impossible to have these days. We're stuck between the polar extremes, with one side screaming at the other side who isn't even listening, while most of us exist somewhere in between. No one is telling the complete truth about the climate, and trying to find a path towards responsible climate policies and practical solutions was just elusive. I started to advocate for something down the middle aisle, where we talk openly about what we know and don't know, along real solutions that we can afford. *Climaturity* became a rallying cry for this new approach.

Q. You shared with me early on that your daughter had come to you in fear and the impact it had on you was the catalyst for this book.

Maybe this is my DNA from having worked so long in the solar industry, where we were really careful about the story that we told. Early on we were just so proud of the narrative and felt like we were telling the truth and making an important and incremental difference.

We didn't overclaim, we didn't under under-claim, we were just telling people what alternatives would be. Fast forward twenty years, and those messages have morphed into we're-all-going-to-die-by-Thursday.

My daughter's generation is hearing these messages nonstop, literally hearing that she's going to die from climate change before she can grow up and have a life.

I also hear it on campus where I teach from students. They feel hopeless, like why even bother trying to build a life because it won't matter anyway. We've got ten years to reverse the entire planet's decline, so why bother?

These messages are just disheartening, and I got to thinking "how did we fail our children so badly? How did we allow this to be the only message they're hearing"?

Q. Why did you choose to write the book?

This really motivated me to try to develop a new narrative, and let's be honest – we're not making any progress whatsoever on the climate. We've spent trillions on so-called solutions that haven't made a dent, the rhetoric has gotten more divisive and apocalyptic, and the only tangible results are scared children and really expensive and ineffective climate policies. Yelling isn't working, panicking isn't working, scaring children isn't working, throwing money at incomplete solutions isn't working, and our climate problem is getting worse and worse. By all measures it's just not working, so we need a new way to approach it.

Right now, the whole process is really just one side yelling at the other side, who isn't even listening. We've got proposed policies that are spending trillions and will have virtually no impact on the climate.

I decided to just come up with a different way to talk about it, because if we really want to solve this problem it's going to take all of us.

I want to have a reasonable and open dialog about what to do, one that require us giving up our kids' college funds to pay for climate solutions.

They is no shortage of expensive proposals with no real insight into how they're solving the problems.

That's why I decided to write this book, as an attempt to start walking down in the middle saying we need people from both sides of political aisle. We need an open discussion. We need to complete all the half-truths that are out there and understand the limitations of what everyone's telling us.

Q. Would it safe to say that you discovered in your research, there's some self-interest that's working its way into the policies and the recommendations and solutions that we're all paying for?

Of course. One of the advantages I have now is that I don't have a product to sell, even though I've had a product to sell for 20 something years. Everyone is telling us their version of the story. We like to demonize big oil, but I don't know one person who is not using the benefits of big oil. Not one. You can't make any solar modules without lots of oil, you can't make windmills without lots of oil. Fossil fuels are part of our everyday life, part of our modern world, and it's not going anywhere soon. Why can't we just acknowledge that and come up with a real plan?

I see stories about how certain energy sources like solar are the cheapest. I know from my background that it's just this tiny little slice of time, this little snapshot, where that's true. Most of the time, like when the sun goes down, it's not true because a billion dollars can't even power one light bulb when there's no sun.

There are all of these half-truths are out there, and if you stagger them around together you can't get the true story. No one knows what the real story is, how bad it is and what some of the solutions are.

Q. Are we doomed and heading towards this direction of no return?

I think we know that the planet is warming. It's not warming by 20 degrees, but it's showing that in general, things are warming up a couple of degrees. Certainly not tragic. I look at the entire

20th century where the world heated by one degree, and humanity prospered just fine. In fact, we've doubled in population and cured hundreds of diseases and it's not fatal. One degree is not going to destroy the planet and it's certainly not going to make humanity extinct.

We know that temperatures are rising. We can show that CO_2 is rising as well, we can show correlation between those two and the jury is still out as to whether or not one causes the other.
Plus, it makes logical sense that with 8 billion people on the planet we are having an effect on it. But our ability to adapt is extreme, and there aren't billions of people heading towards their imminent death because the climate is turning against us.

Q. Is anyone out there giving us a clear story of what is happening with the climate change?

There's a few. There's a Danish economist named Bjorn Lomborg who's produced of a couple of films and books and has been putting dollar numbers to a lot of these solutions, which I appreciate. In practical terms, if the goal is to save humanity, then there's a lot better ways to spend our money.

Roger Pielke writes about energy policy and the IPCC, typically in Forbes magazine.

Michael Shellenberger is a reformed hardcore environmental activist who's now a nuclear proponent, who often writes for Forbes and the Wall Street Journal.

Q. Can solar windmills, electric vehicles, all these solutions that we're spending billions of dollars on solve the problem of global warming?

That's the question with all of these things - what's going to help?, Will solar help? Of course. Will windmills help? Of course. Will EVs help? Of course. Will they help a lot? No, and there's lots of reasons for that.

Solar was always meant as a supplementary power source, it was always meant to be plugged into the side of the existing grid to just help give it some flexibility and some "cleanness" if that's the right word. But now it's being promoted as climate salvation and you know, how can a resource that works only 30% of the time be something that you can rely on?

It's not a replacement, it never will be. People say, well let's add batteries, which means we're digging up the earth for a different type of energy, just replacing one type of depleting resource with another.

Look if we solarized the planet, if we switched everyone over to EVs tomorrow, would we meet any of our goals? No, we wouldn't even come close. And the math is really simple. That's what frustrates me about a lot of this and why I started down this path, which is that dollars matter, dollars per CO_2 reduced matter.

We have to be having that discussion. If we spend $2 trillion on electric vehicles, will it get us towards our goal? Almost not at all. The best thing we can do for that is just driving less.

Q. Is public transportation a good alternative?

Yes. Oddly enough, the best thing that happened to the climate was COVID. In 2020, we cut our emissions as a country by 11%, 15% in transportation. In one year, we did what 45 years of aggressive climate policy couldn't do. We did it in months by just using less stuff.

The cheapest and quickest way to lower emissions is through conservation. Turn off lights, drive less, use less stuff, don't replace that TV. Find ways to not do more. And imagine if governments had policies in place to incentivize us to save resources, to actually pay us to conserve electricity and water. Utilities already do this when they're anticipating heat waves and such that could cause blackouts, so the mechanisms are already in-place.

And then there's hundreds of natural solutions like trees and carbon sequestration that we just are completely ignoring. In terms of the dollar impact they're much better and easier to implement.

Q. If lowering CO_2 is the goal, what solutions are the best?

The goal of all our climate activities is temperature mitigation, and by proxy, CO_2 reduction. We need to lower total CO_2 levels. Conservation is the quickest and fastest way to do that. Energy efficiency is also important, helping buildings use less resources. Then there are the hundreds of natural solutions like reforestation and agri-farming and soil replenishment that all capture and sequester carbon. Then we need to be developing and deploying carbon capture technologies as quickly as we can.

The main problem I have with massive decarbonization is that it still continues to add CO_2 into the atmosphere. All energy sources emit CO_2, so replacing capacity at a coal plant with solar, for example, can potentially reduce future CO_2 emissions, but solar still has a CO_2 footprint and therefore increases total CO_2 levels.

That's where we get into this funny *climaccounting* gray area, where we replace some bad energy source with something better that might yield benefits over time – but those savings vary based on dozens of factors and we can never prove them. There is no such thing as a neutral energy source – solar, wind, batteries, coal, gas, nuclear all have CO_2 footprints – so the idea of replacing one energy source with another and hoping to lower total CO_2 is fiction.

Adaptation doesn't get talked about much as a response to climate change, but it's a realistic approach to handle it. It doesn't spend trillions to try and lower CO_2, it acknowledges it will rise at some level and that humanity will adapt. Every species adapts to climate fluctuations already, and we're no different.

A great example is New Orleans, where Hurricane Katrina ravaged the city in 2007 and killed thousands; in 2021 Hurricane Ida slammed the city but caused 150 deaths. What changed?

They rebuilt the levee system after it collapsed during Katrina, which prevented further deaths with Ida. Instead of relying on trillions to lower global temperatures, New Orleans adapted to their local conditions.

Q. You introduced me to this concept of climate credits. Is it driven by politicians and public policy?

I don't know how many people understand how climate credits really work and how companies are being given incentives and how they can purchase credits from other companies. But is that an example of where the politicians and the policies are just sending us on this trajectory, in the wrong direction.

The idea with climate credits is you can buy someone else's right to pollute. This is typically when governments decide they're going to regulate their emissions, they put a cap and trade like we've done in California.

Q. They penalize you financially if you pollute too much?

That's cap and trade. You're allowed to emit a certain amount of CO_2 from your operations, and if you go above that you're penalized. The way that you get around that is you buy that excess pollution space from other companies.

I personally am in favor of financial markets like this, because it starts to put price tags on climate change. It gives companies financial incentives to emit less, which is a good thing. It can work, but like everything, it just depends on the implementation and who oversees and manages the program.

Look, people have to be able to make money at it. Making money is not a terrible thing. We're not going to completely gut the entire economy in order to reverse climate change, it's just not going to happen. People have to have jobs, things have to make financial sense. I personally don't care about demonizing oil companies because I've seen what happens when they focus attention on solving problems. If you can show them a way to make money by pulling carbon out of the air, watch what happens. Watch all those resources get focused into actually making things better.

Q. Companies can use climate credits in their business model?

The biggest one I can think of is Tesla. Since they produce only electric vehicles, they're given carbon credits and yes, they can trade them to other companies who need them. In 2021 Tesla earned more than $500 million in carbon credit revenue. It's a huge part of their business, one you don't hear much about.

The global carbon trading market set to be one of the hottest industries in the next 30 years, for all these reasons. It has potential to be fraudulent, like any other financial transaction, but it's getting a lot of attention right now and it's a viable business.

Q. The goal for California at a very high level is to get to this place called net zero, right? Is that a realistic goal?

Whether or not it's a realistic goal depends on the solutions they're going to implement and the amount of money they're going to spend. We certainly won't get there with public EV charging stations and green-painted bike lanes. But even if we find enough money, I question whether or not it's even the right goal.

Net zero has become synonymous with climate salvation, but think about what it really means. Net zero means that we're going to zero out the growth of our CO_2 problem, not eliminate it. It just means we're going to slow down its growth over a long period of time, and with a great deal of expense.

I call net zero the avoided donut fallacy. Imagine your doctor said you had to lose 100 pounds or else you'd suffer severe health consequences. You're used to eating 20 donuts a day, so you decide to stop eating those 20 donuts a day. Great! But did you get skinny from doing that? No, you just stopped yourself from getting fatter. You can't use an 'avoid donuts' strategy to slimness, you still have to lose those 100 pounds. Net zero is the equivalent of avoiding those 20 donuts per day.

Even after we spend the trillions and the decades it will take to get to net zero, we still have to lose the weight; we still have to remove total CO_2 from the atmosphere. That's why net zero is, in a sense, fool's gold: it makes us think we've hit the climate jackpot when, in reality, we still haven't solved the problem.

Wouldn't a better strategy be to not stop at net zero but actually go carbon negative? Microsoft has committed to doing just that. They've committed to actually removing all of the carbon they've emitted since their company beg in the 1970s, not just stopping its growth in 20 years. That's a real commitment. How and whether or not they get there remain to be seen, but I applaud the commitment. That's what it's going to take.

By the way, in our donut scenario, installing solar or switching to EVs is like going from eating 20 donuts per day to 5, then taking credit for saving 15 donuts. Either way you're still 5 donuts fatter tomorrow than you are today.

Back to your original question, are net zero realistic goals? Maybe after decades and great expense, but they're the wrong goals.

Q. We can do everything right here in the U S which we have control over, but ultimately, aren't we are all impacted by the actions of other countries who are struggling to get their own economies under way, but not being playing by the same rules?

I would love to see the U.S. lead this with a brand-new approach. Again, this is why I wrote this book, to try and begin a different dialog about it all. We need only do we need a collective policy, but also a collective ethos, one that's based on truth and transparency.

I would love to see us do this as a country. Just say, here's the way we're going to tackle this, we're going to be open about it, we're going to talk about the limitations of climate science, what's real, what's not.

Here are the things that we're guessing at, here are all the options that are available to us, the pluses and minuses. Is it really an emergency? If so, then why isn't anyone driving to the emergency room? And if it isn't, quit saying it. Hell, we all have collective boy-who-cried-wolf-syndrome anyway.

Here's how much money we think we can reasonably spend and then create a real model that we can look at and say, all right, developing nations, here's something that we can report. Because developing nations, they need guidance. They need a blueprint.

Developing nations are not going to give up oil. They need reliable energy, something they can count on, so a total reliance on intermittent energy is never going to happen. They need a reasonable path to prosperity, and us First World nations are the only ones to give it.

We need to create a blueprint that's manageable and doesn't require a complete reversal of everyone's way of life in order to make it work. I would love to see us work towards something like that.

Q. Do we need to have full disclosure if we stand to benefit from the solutions we recommend?

It needs to be transparent to everybody because you have to question the policy should be being made by people have there's no bias and full disclosure is means you kind of lay out all of your cards. And then we know for sure that you're coming from a place of truth, because I think what's ultimately happening is there's just a lot of bias that people carry into this conversation that they don't even realize they have.

Q. And implicit bias too?

Look, we all have biases, I know I certainly do.

My view on energy options is we need them all. I mean, oil is not going to anywhere in our lifetimes, and for those who have this need to rid the world of fossil fuels then I invite them to quite using those products today, just like you would any other product you don't like. It's certainly your right to do that. But to expect that the world will follow you is a bit ridiculous, don't you think?

It takes a lot of oil and gas to make products that use less oil and gas. Every single thing that we have - shoes, clothing, food, the microphone that this is being recorded on - is made with oil. We need it forever. It's not going away and it doesn't need to, but that doesn't mean we can't make a cleaner transition. But is all this yelling and screaming fear-mongering helping? My belief is that it's grinding climate progress to a halt.

We're not killing our kids. We're just not, they're going to be able to have kids.

Q. Are we using fear as a lever for change?

Writing the book itself was actually eye opening in a lot of ways, because I did a lot of research and uncovered that these are actual strategies.

It didn't happen by coincidence. If you're wondering where the media got this from, I can show you the blueprint. There's a labeling guide that says here's what you should call people if they don't agree with you, you're not allowed to say climate skeptic, they have to call you a climate science denier. This is Columbia university's journalism school, here is the blueprint.

Scared kids can't be the goal, scared kids just leads us to all this ineffective stuff. You don't want to force people to choose between their college education and saving the planet because guaranteed, everyone's going to put their kids into college. It'll never happen. So how about reasonable stuff that will actually make an impact, with results we can actually show.

ENDNOTES

[1] https://en.wikipedia.org/wiki/Intergovernmental_Panel_on_Climate_Chan ge

[2] https://www.forbes.com/sites/rogerpielke/2019/12/06/the-incredible-story-of-how-climate-change-became-apocalyptic/?sh=2e47099c789d

[3] ipcc.ch/site/assets/uploads/2018/03/sres-en.pdf

[4] In 2021, IPCC AR6 added 5 new scenarios into the mix, bringing the total to 45. While I describe the scenario strategy using the previous number 40, the same logic applies to the new 45.

[5] By RCraig09 – Own work, CC BY-SA 4.0, https://commons.wikimedia.org/w/index.php?curid=88535596

[6] Temperature measurement and its history is a complex scientific journey, and I won't go into the pros/cons of each type of analysis; frankly, it's beyond my scientific capabilities. I'm simply presenting a summary to help frame our discussion.

[7] By Femke Nijsse - Own work, CC BY-SA 3.0, https://commons.wikimedia.org/w/index.php?curid=69480542

[8] By Renerpho - Own work, CC BY-SA 4.0, https://commons.wikimedia.org/w/index.php?curid=78909796

[9] https://www.ncdc.noaa.gov/global-warming/temperature-change

[10] https://phys.org/news/2012-07-temperatures-co2-climate.html

[11] https://justfacts.votesmart.org/public-statement/369466/issue-position-climate-change-and-policy-implications/#.XZkxXS-ZMWp

[12] https://skepticalscience.com/co2-lags-temperature.htm

[13] https://www.sunysuffolk.edu/explore-academics/faculty-and-staff/faculty-websites/scott-mandia/global_warming/global_warming_misinformation_co2_lags_not_le ads.html

[14] https://www.sciencedirect.com/science/article/pii/S0921818112001658

[15] https://www.dailymail.co.uk/news/article-2419557/Climate-change-models-accurate-study-finds-widely-overestimated-global-warming.html

[16] https://www.sciencemag.org/news/2019/04/new-climate-models-predict-warming-surge

[17] https://www.vox.com/energy-and-environment/2019/12/4/20991315/climate-change-prediction-models-accurate

[18] https://www.cato.org/sites/cato.org/files/pubs/pdf/working-paper-35_2.pdf

[19] https://co2coalition.org/frequently-asked-questions/#1465245604826-64586917-ba84

[20] https://www.carbonbrief.org/analysis-how-well-have-climate-models-projected-global-warming

[21] https://www.forbes.com/sites/startswithabang/2017/03/15/the-first-climate-model-turns-50-and-predicted-global-warming-almost-perfectly/?sh=6db68e1c6614

[22] http://co2coalition.org/2020/11/24/an-exchange-on-climate-science-and-alarm/

[23] https://www.ipcc.ch/site/assets/uploads/2017/08/AR5_Uncertainty_Guidance_Note.pdf

[24] https://www.merriam-webster.com/dictionary/science

[25] https://grist.org/article/roberts2/

[26] https://rebellion.global/

[27] https://twitter.com/billmckibben/status/1198375629638586373?s=20

[28] https://www.vice.com/en/article/8xwygg/the-collapse-of-civilization-may-have-already-begun

[29] https://www.usatoday.com/story/news/politics/onpolitics/2019/01/22/ocasio-cortez-climate-change-alarm/2642481002/

[30] https://apnews.com/article/bd45c372caf118ec99964ea547880cd0

[31] https://nobluedawn.com/?p=2246

[32] https://iopscience.iop.org/article/10.1088/1674-4527/21/6/131/pdf

[33] https://www.forbes.com/sites/rogerpielke/2019/12/06/the-incredible-story-of-how-climate-change-became-apocalyptic/?sh=2e47099c789d

[34] https://issues.org/the-trouble-with-climate-emergency-journalism/

[35] https://www.imf.org/en/Publications/WP/Issues/2019/05/02/Global-Fossil-Fuel-Subsidies-Remain-Large-An-Update-Based-on-Country-Level-Estimates-46509

[36] https://www.forbes.com/sites/bjornlomborg/2020/01/17/the-imfs-huge-miscalculation-of-energy-subsidies/?sh=670d74f74b42

[37] https://bcse.org/factbook/#

[38] http://energypost.eu/jobs-investing-in-renewables-beats-fossil-fuels/

[39] https://www.washingtonpost.com/magazine/2020/02/03/eco-anxiety-is-overwhelming-kids-wheres-line-between-education-alarmism/?arc404=true

[40] https://www.forbes.com/sites/michaelshellenberger/2019/12/04/why-climate-alarmism-hurts-us-all/?sh=6b8cef3d36d8

[41] Extinction Rebellion, XR is an environmental group founded to commit civil disobedience to draw awareness to the threat of climate change.

[42] https://www.independent.co.uk/news/world/europe/extinction-rebellion-founder-roger-hallam-holocaust-genocide-nazis-a9211781.html

[43] https://www.thenation.com/article/archive/how-do-you-decide-to-have-a-baby-when-climate-change-is-remaking-life-on-earth/

[44] https://nationalpost.com/life/is-it-immoral-to-have-babies-in-the-era-of-climate-change

[45] https://www.npr.org/2016/08/18/479349760/should-we-be-having-kids-in-the-age-of-climate-change

[46] http://web.archive.org/web/20160307123411/https://www3.epa.gov/climatechange/endangerment/

[47] https://co2coalition.org/co2-fundamentals/

[48] https://skepticalscience.com/co2-pollutant-advanced.htm

[49] By RCraig09 – Own work, CC BY-SA 4.0, https://commons.wikimedia.org/w/index.php?curid=88535596

[50] https://ourworldindata.org/crop-yields

[51] https://financialpost.com/opinion/bjorn-lomborg-climate-change-and-deaths-from-extreme-heat-and-cold

[52] Climateattribution.org

53
https://climate.law.columbia.edu/sites/default/files/content/docs/The%2
0Law%20and%20Science%20of%20Climate%20Change%20Attribution_B
urger%2C%20Wentz%20%26%20Horton.pdf

[54] https://www.carbonbrief.org/carbon-brief-interview-michael-gerrard

[55] https://cleantechrising.com/whats-the-difference-between-carbon-neutral-zero-carbon-and-negative-emissions/

[56] https://carbon.ci/insights/companies-with-net-zero-targets/

[57] https://www.wsj.com/graphics/are-electric-cars-really-better-for-the-environment/36

[58] Here are the calculations: 200 trillion kilowatt-hours is 200,000,000,000,000,000 watt-hours of energy needed; divide that by 8 hours to get 25,000,000,000,000,000 watts, or 25 terrawatts. Subtract installed solar capacity of 750,000,000,000 watts, to get 24,999,250,000,000 watts needed. Divide that number by 140,000,000,000 of global solar manufacturing capacity, and we get 178.56.

[59] https://www.nrel.gov/analysis/life-cycle-assessment.html (chart generated by M. Cortez, using NREL data)

[60] http://stacks.iop.org/ERL/8/024024

[61] https://www.washingtonpost.com/climate-solutions/2020/06/29/climate-change-racism/

[62] https://www.dailywire.com/news/buttigieg-claims-racism-is-physically-built-into-u-s-interstate-system

[63] wri.org/carbonremoval

[64] Drawdown.org

Made in the USA
Columbia, SC
23 July 2022